FINDING GOD

BETWEEN A ROCK & A HARD PLACE

STORIES OF

GRATITUDE & GRACE

COMPILED BY LIL COPAN & ELISA FRYLING

HAROLD SHAW PUBLISHERS, WHEATON, ILLINOIS

ISBN 0-87788-329-7

Cover design and illustration by David LaPlaca

Library of Congress Cataloging-in-Publication Data

Finding God between a rock and a hard place : stories of gratitude and grace / compiled by Lil Copan and Elisa Fryling.

p. cm.

ISBN 0-87788-329-7 (pbk.)

1. Prayer—Christianity. I. Copan, Lil. II. Fryling, Elisa.

1976– .

BV220.F56 1999

248.4—dc21 099-23194

CIP

---

03 02 01 00 99

7 6 5 4 3 2 1

Table of Contents

Introduction

God's grace is not far off; it is here with us in our stories. It is in the stories of the obscure and the famous, the confident and the powerless, the ones who seek God and expect to find and the ones who are unaware of what they seek.

These stories remind us how bright the kingdom of God is here and now. Writer after writer tells us remarkable personal experiences of answered prayer and signs of grace. God seems to "show up" when we witness acts of kindness. A healing, a hope restored, or a light in the darkness remind us of God's love. We long to treasure the miraculous—these glimpses of God—in our hearts.

Every day, God writes stories of grace for us. In this book we see a small reflection of how God is at work. We can respond in gratitude as we see that the gracious God behind each story is the gracious God behind each of our lives.

All in Good Time

[God's persistence] has all the surprise and creativity,

and yet all the certainty and regularity, of a new day.

Sunrise—when the spontaneous and the certain

arrive at the same time. Does anyone ever get used to daybreak?

EUGENE PETERSON, RUN WITH THE HORSES

CHAPTER ONE

God's Gracious Timing

Sometimes our timing is different from God's,
but God's timing is always perfect.

Mama's Pride*

JO KADLECEK

It wasn't a crowded plane. Seats were uncommonly empty, like the stares of these early morning passengers. This would be a quiet flight, a sleepy one, where career agendas and hard good-byes would fade into three hours of unconscious travel.

Then the teenage mother with stringy hair, thick glasses, and rose-red lips walked on board. She smiled softly as she slipped through first class and into her seat back in 21D. Baby son—barely a year—was already working his mama over on this cold, quiet November morning. One seat wasn't enough for his baby blue eyes and so he wandered through 22 and 23 and back again to 21D, his tiny hands and knees in perpetual motion.

It was fun at first for Baby, and Mama kept smiling as flight attendants and businessmen cooed and cuddled him. But after take-off and orange juice and banana bread, Baby's vocal chords unfastened like the seat belts of confident passengers. Young Mama was patient, following, playing, singing, praying for anything to calm her bellowing son. The plastic pink pacifier was not enough for this wiggly, tired boy. No warm milk, no clapping games, no emergency exit cards in the seat pocket in front of them could hold his attention, or his hollers.

Stares darted past the coffee cart. Headsets went on. Little pillows and blue blankets fell over ears. Still, Mama smiled and held on for life. She was a fighter. "He is a good boy," her face apologized to anyone who glared at the noise. "My son doesn't usually cry like this. . . ."

Her silent speech, and her attempts to harness one-year-old energy, were interrupted by old, worn hands from across the aisle. The elderly woman's blue eyes matched Baby's. "He's a good boy," said the frail seventy-something woman in 22C. Her wrinkled face made more wrinkles as she threw a laugh and a kiss to Mama's pride. Fragile but firm arms underneath brown embroidered sweater (the kind that anyone else would have given to the Salvation Army) reached across to 21D, picked up the boy, and drew him close to her.

And then a tiny miracle occurred on Flight 134.

Silence suddenly resounded throughout the cabin as thick as the baby wails that had pierced it only seconds before. Fingers barely bigger than a knitting needle began tracing the brown flowers on the elderly woman's chest. She cooed at him and whispered to him and held him tight. She rocked him and walked him and talked him all the way to first class and back.

"Take a break, honey," said one generation to another, one tired mother to another. Familiarity, like an old favorite sweater, comforted the younger caregiver, and the soft teenage smile flashed compliance to the wisdom standing before her. And for the first time in a long time, the aged woman felt . . . useful.

And so affection soothed both the one-year-old bundle and the wrinkled life holding him. So much so that baby boy finally, happily, slept. Mama rested. Elderly bones felt human again.

And absolute strangers became family for a simple, satisfying moment.

Thanking God for Rats

BARBARA GRIFFITHS

While a missionary in Thailand, I had little money for food, transportation, or other needs. One afternoon when I was particularly discouraged I began looking for Sunday school materials in a desk drawer. I pulled open the drawer and there before my eyes was a huge mess. The drawer had become a rat's nest, with mother rat and five babies staring at me. Mother and babies disappeared in a flash, and then I sat on the floor with the drawer beside me and looked at the mess. I could have cried.

"Oh Lord, it's not fair," I told him. "This is too much! There's so much to do today and now I have to clear this up and I still don't have any money to go on to the next village tomorrow."

Every bit of paper in the drawer had become part of the rat's nest, and I began scooping it out and putting it in the rubbish basket. Everything had been chewed to mincemeat to make the nest, except for one envelope halfway down in the back left-hand corner. I nearly threw it straight in the rubbish basket. But thinking I'd better check that it was empty, I pulled it open. Inside was enough money in the local currency for all the rest of my trip. God had provided money in his own way and time. I never knew that one day I would be thanking the Lord for rats!

God's Timing Was Right

DAVID SCOTT

My wife Jane died of cancer several years ago. I had prayed hard for her healing. After her death I was so hurt that I couldn't even pray for about three years.

After eleven years as a widower, I had begun thinking about remarriage. But I wasn't very good at dating! During those years as a widower, however, my path had crossed that of Nancy Fox, an old friend of Jane's.

Nancy and I had never discussed moving beyond our casual friendship, but then circumstances offered us the opportunity to spend two weekends together. During that time we shared with each other our stories, talked about our families, discussed the Bible together—and wondered if our friendship could lead to marriage. We also discussed Jane's death and my struggles during that time. It was a big decision, but we realized that the natural next step to take was marriage. We both sensed God's timing was right and decided to be in love.

As Nancy and I made calls to out-of-town friends to let them know we were engaged, I called Kathy in Oregon. She had been a good friend of Jane's. I told her whom I was marrying. There was silence on the other end of the line. Finally, she said, "I don't know her, but I know her name." Kathy went on to explain that she had heard Jane talk about Nancy on several occasions over the years. The February before Jane died, Jane and Kathy had met at a writers' conference in Illinois. Jane was very sick and they knew it would be the last time they would see each other, so their conversations were poignant. Jane mentioned Nancy's name again, telling Kathy that the one person she could see me with after her death was Nancy Fox.

Although Jane had told me that she had picked out the person she wanted me to marry, she wouldn't tell me who it was. Sometimes God will allow difficulties to accomplish his objectives. I don't think of this story as how God answers our prayers, because God's answer to our prayer for Jane's healing was no. But I think of this story with Nancy as one of God's timing and his grace and providence. He didn't heal Jane, but now I can see clearly how he was at work in my life.

No More, No Less

SUSAN NELSON

The Saturday following New Year's, my husband and I were scheduled to travel with our three-month-old son and sixteen-month-old daughter from our vacation in Florida to our home in Minnesota. Our flight was scheduled to connect through Detroit. We awoke that morning and watched the Weather Channel. We knew storms were brewing in the Midwest but hoped to get home safely later that day. As a concerned mother, I packed extra diapers, formula, and a sweater for my two children.

We left Florida without any complications. Space was tight, since we had only two seats for my husband, two children, and me. We arrived in Detroit and changed planes with little time to spare. Once we were on our connecting flight the plane pulled away from the gate on time, and five hours later we were still sitting on the runway about one mile from our gate, waiting to take off. The storm we had watched on the Weather Channel was now our reality. My husband and I kept passing our babies back and forth, and I was getting anxious since we were running out of diapers and formula. The pilot kept giving us hourly updates to let us know that we were waiting for the plane to get de-iced, but the equipment and planes were getting stuck in the snow. The plane only had peanuts, pretzels, and pop for us to eat, and those quickly ran out.

After our five-hour wait on the runway, at 11:00 P.M., the pilot finally taxied us back to the terminal and we were able to get off the plane and re-enter the airport. The FAA closed the Detroit airport and said flights would hopefully resume around noon the next day. Things were chaotic at the airport since there were thousands of stranded travelers like ourselves. Burger King and Pizza Hut had both run out of burgers and pizza. My husband and I would have gladly settled for a candy bar, but our first concern was to locate food and diapers for our babies.

After we searched over an hour for help in finding diapers and formula, God led us to a club waiting room for world travelers. I went to the information desk at the club and started crying as I described how I was searching for formula and diapers for my baby. The attendant said she would be off work in a few minutes and then she would help us search. As a weary traveler, mother, and wife, I felt the need to call my mom and ask her to start praying for us. She prayed with me over the phone and asked the Lord to bring us someone who could locate the needed food and diapers. When we prayed that prayer, I was anticipating that the Lord would give us some way—maybe a 4-wheel drive Jeep or snowplow—to get to a convenience store near the airport so I could purchase the supplies. Talking and praying with my mom calmed my heart and gave me the grace to tend to the needs of my family.

Since our baby bottles were empty, I needed to rinse them out in the ladies' restroom of this club. As I was cleaning out the bottles, I started talking to other ladies in the restroom and began crying when I mentioned that I didn't have food for my babies. The lady at the sink next to me had just finished expressing breast milk, as she was also stranded, and away from her four-month-old baby. She kindly asked me if she could help us out by giving us bottles of her breast milk so I could feed my baby. She said that she was healthy, a registered dietitian, and she would love to help out. She had just gotten off the phone with her husband and was feeling helpless being away from her baby and not able to use the breast milk she was producing. We were each an answer to the other's prayers.

By God's grace and mercy, his servant gave us enough breast milk for my son and milk and juice for my daughter to get us through the next fourteen hours. We had just enough milk to last until we were able to go to a grocery store near the airport back home. My three-month-old son had no reaction to the breast milk. The airline was able to locate some extra diapers for both my children. My husband and I realized that we were never hungry throughout this experience until our plane landed in Minneapolis . . . again, God's grace was sufficient and we didn't need food when our children did. Being stranded in an airport without food, diapers, or warm clothes, our prayers were answered and God physically gave us exactly (no more and no less than) what we needed to get safely through a blizzard with our children.

The Empty Basket

PATRICIA ST. JOHN

We met Mr. Maltar in the strange and beautiful place where for many years he worked as keeper—the Garden Tomb in Jerusalem. In this place a single old tomb is cut in the face of the rock, and there is a single slab of stone inside where a body was once laid. Outside are the grooves of a great boulder that must once have been rolled across the entrance. There is no stone there now; the grave is open and empty. Because of its structure and position, many people think that this must be the tomb which Joseph of Arimathea gave for the burial of Jesus.

Many tourists come to see the garden tomb, and Mr. Maltar, the Arab guardian, used to love to show such visitors round the quiet, beautifully kept garden and talk to them about the gospel story.

When we met him, he invited us to a meal, and we asked him how he and his wife had come to be in charge of this place and whether he had been there long. So he told us his story.

Until the time of the partition when Jerusalem was divided into Arab and Jewish sections, Mr. Maltar had been a bank manager. When war broke out, he and his wife and nine children were away from home and, on account of the fighting, were unable to get back. His bank, his house, and all his money were in an area allocated to the Jews, and he and his family were stranded and fast becoming destitute.

"Daily I went to the branch of our bank situated in Jerusalem," he said, "but no money was coming through, and they could not help me. At home we had lived comfortably; my children had never lacked anything. But here in Jerusalem our money was running out fast, and my wife and I were getting worried. Later there was relief organized for the hundreds of refugees, but just then all was in confusion. We did not know where to turn for help.

"But daily we turned to the Lord. We read his promises to ourselves, and we gathered our children and read the promises to them. We read in the Psalms, 'The young lions do lack and suffer hunger but those who seek the Lord will not be wanting any good thing.' We read in Isaiah, 'God's people will be free from worries, and their homes peaceful and safe. How happy everyone will be with plenty of water for the crops and safe pasture.' Most of all we trusted the words of Jesus: 'Be concerned above everything else with the Kingdom of God and with what he requires of you, and he will provide you with all other things.'

"I felt quite sure that God would keep his promises and we would not go hungry. But I wanted my children to be sure of this, too. The day came when we finished the last of our food for breakfast, and once again I spoke to them. 'Children,' I said. 'The Lord has promised to give us what we need, but we have no money and no dinner. So we will tell this to the Lord and to no one else. And I will go out with this empty basket and you will stay at home. Then we shall see whether the promises of God are true or not.'

"So we all prayed round the empty basket. The children understood that this was very important, and they watched me walk down the street with the empty basket in my hand. I did not know where to go, but I decided to look in at the branch of our bank again in case anything was coming through.

"The answer was the same as before. As I turned to go, I found an old friend of mine from my home town in the queue. He had left the district before the worst troubles and banked his money in Jerusalem.

"'Why, Maltar!' cried my friend. 'What are you doing here?'

"'We have a small house in Jerusalem,' I replied, 'and we were on holiday. We were not able to get back home.'

"'Then you must be having money problems. Tell me, how are you managing?'

"I was about to tell him of our plight when I remembered my words to the children. 'We will tell the Lord and no one else,' I had said. So I told him we were quite all right and left the bank with my empty basket. I did not know where to go next, so I went and sat on a seat in the shade in the park opposite. *I spoke the truth,* I thought to myself. *Those who trust in God are always all right. All will be well.*

"I sat staring at the ground waiting for a word or a sign. I did not hear when my old friend walked toward me across the grass. 'I don't care what you say, Maltar. You can't be all right with nine kids to feed.' he said. Then he dropped a handful of bank notes into the empty basket and went on his way.

"I rose up and went to the market and filled the basket until it was almost too heavy to carry. I bought all that we needed for a good lunch and much more, and the rest of the money I put in my pocket. Then I went home. It was nearly lunch time, and the children were waiting at the gate. They stared in wonder at the overflowing basket.

"Then we sat down together and ate our meal. It was good to eat so bountifully after the lean week that had passed, but it was even better to know that the Lord keeps his promises."

Shortly after this, Mr. Maltar found work, and after his children grew up, he and his wife retired to the little bungalow built in the garden of the resurrection. He became keeper of the tomb and the garden until the Six Days' War when he was shot dead, right by the open door of the grave. Perhaps he, who loved the place so much, would have been glad to die on the very spot where his master conquered death.

The Ring

KIM BOLTON WITH CHRIS WAVE

One spring, I realized I was missing a ring. It wasn't an expensive ring, but my husband, Tony, had given it to me when we first got married. It was a sentimental thing.

I called everyone I knew to see if I had left it anywhere. I called my mom. "Did I take that ring off while I was doing dishes at your house?"

"No," she said.

Nobody had seen that ring. "That ring is somewhere, Lord. I know you know where it is. Would you please get it to show up? When I find it, I'll be like the woman in the parable with the lost coin. I'm going to shout my find from the rooftops. I'm going to call all my friends and family. I've already called all of them to sweep out their houses. Now I'm just gonna wait."

Summer came and went, and I put all thoughts of the ring in the back of my mind. In September, Tony and I had a string of musical engagements in north Atlanta. We packed the family in the van—four kids, two car seats, two strollers, two diaper bags, two of everything. Videos, tapes, games, toys, and food, all packed in the van, and electronic equipment in the trailer behind it.

We sang Friday night, Saturday night, Sunday morning, and Sunday night. Every engagement was in a different place. To get the girls back home and into school Monday morning, we needed to leave Atlanta by nine. We knew the route and the routine. With the kids asleep in the car, we'd get home by three, sleep till six, and the kids could catch the school bus at seven. Perfect.

"Right on schedule," Tony said. And then, "Kim, do you hear that noise?"

"What noise?"

"I think we have a flat tire." He was listening to the bumping sound carefully. "It's a flat on the trailer, and I don't have a spare for the trailer. There's a gas station. If it's a real gas station it won't take long at all."

We pulled off the exit and drove right to the station. It was a food store, not a real gas station. I wasn't worried. Tony can fix anything. I figured he'd duct tape it if he had to.

Before we knew it, however, there were eight big guys surrounding the van and trailer. One man had a glazed-over look and was sweating profusely on this chilly evening. The smell of alcohol surrounded the van. The men forcefully offered us their help. Several times. Tony thanked them each time and said he could handle it. Ignoring his refusals of assistance, they took the spare tire off of the van. Then they started to take the trailer tire off. Right before our eyes they began to strip our van and trailer.

One of them asked for money for helping with the tire change. Tony thought we'd better give him some. As Tony came up to the van window to get money, he said to me, "Kimberly, it's time to pray. Make sure all the doors are locked."

All four of the children were asleep. I prayed, "Lord, please send an angel. Do something, Lord. I'm not even sure what's going on out there. I don't want them to know I've got four children in this van."

One of the guys kept asking Tony, "What've you got in that trailer? What kinda stuff's in there?"

"Nothing much. Just stuff."

"Let's see if there's anything in the trailer to pull out and fix this thing." While one man distracted Tony, the others tried to get into the back of the trailer.

"Listen, I'm going to call a wrecker," said Tony. "I don't need any help. Thank you."

Right about that time (it was eleven o'clock), the gas station lights went off. They closed and locked up. The place went pitch dark. It was happening so fast. Eight guys surrounding Tony and the van. The girls woke up. "What's the matter, Mom?"

"Well, nothing yet. Your dad's trying to fix a tire."

"Looks like he has a lot of help out there."

"I know it looks like it, but they're not really helping."

"Are we in trouble, Mom?"

At this point, we would have driven on the tire rim if we could have gotten out of there. But we couldn't. We were stuck. The wheel was already off the trailer, and the situation was rapidly getting worse. The man who seemed to be on drugs started talking faster and faster. Two others began arguing about who was there first and who should get the money.

"Amber, what was your verse in school this week?" I asked my daughter.

"'Put on the whole armor of God.'"

"Okay, let's put on our helmet, that breastplate, tie tight your shoes of peace. Here's another one. 'God didn't give us a spirit of fear, but power, love, and a sound mind.' Girls, we need to concentrate on what God can do for us. And right now we need him to step in and get us out of here." And then I prayed, "God, give us creative wisdom to know what to do."

All at once, I remembered the cell phone. Underneath all the baby gear was the new cell phone! Trying not to sound afraid or excited, I dialed the operator. "Hello, I'm at exit 11, the Dorcet exit on

I-65. We are surrounded by eight guys we don't know. My husband is outside and I'm inside our van with our four children. We are not in an emergency situation yet but I would like for someone to come. Someone with authority. Someone official, with a car that has a blue light. My children are in the vehicle. Do you have children? Do you understand what I'm trying to say?"

"Yes, I understand." There was a long pause. "But you're not at exit 11 on I-65. There is no Dorcet exit on I-65."

"I'm *telling* you I'm looking at the sign. I know this route well. I'm coming from Atlanta to Fort Walton Beach. I'm at exit 11. Please, I have four children. Do you have children?"

"Yes, I have children, but you're not on I-65."

"Where am I?"

"Could you be on I-85?"

"*Yes! I'm on I-85.* I am coming from Atlanta headed south. I have not yet made it to Montgomery."

"I'll have someone right there. Let me transfer you to the Dorcet police department. I'll be thinking about you." Something about her kind manner comforted me. She transferred me straight in.

A voice answered slow and lazy, "Off..ic..er Graaanspaugh." Of course, I had to be talking to the one officer who seemed to have all the time in the world. I wanted to scream.

"Hello, sir," I said and went through the whole thing again: "I have four children in my van and we're surrounded by eight men. I'm not in trouble yet, but it looks like there's going to be trouble. Could you please send some authority? Soon?"

Another slow response. "Yeeees . . . Where . . . might . . . ya'll . . . beee?"

"Exit 11, I-85, at the gas station up on the hill."

Even more slowly, and drawling every word, he said, "IIII'll seeeeend . . . someooooone . . . out diiiirectly."

Ninety seconds later, a car pulled up, lights flashing, gravel spitting on the pavement, and Officer Barney Fife jumped out. He looked straight at Tony and said, "I don't need any trouble. I'm retiring in two weeks and do you know what kind of paperwork an incident like this requires?"

Tony replied, "These guys are all over my van. I can't get them out of here. I need some help."

The man who seemed to be on drugs said to the police officer, "I've got a gun."

"I've got a gun, too, Joe." Barney replied. He obviously knew the man.

"No," Joe said, "I don't wan . . . I don't wan . . . you . . . give me any trouble." Back and forth the talk and guns went, all around my kids and my van, with my husband in the middle of it. The cop wooed the drug-crazed guy away, saying, "Come on over here, Joe. Come on, get over here."

As the officer pulled the guy away Tony came to the van and said, "Kimberly, is there a coat in the van? It's getting cold." September is not usually cold in the south.

My daughter found a jacket underneath the back seat of the van. Tony slipped it on. Joe and Barney Fife were now having it out in front of us. The tension was thick. Tony came back to the van with a smile on his face. "Look what I found in the pocket of this jacket!"

I looked. "Hey girls, " I said. "You can go back to sleep. Jesus just showed up."

In front of me was my gold ring.

If God cared so much about my gold ring that cost nearly nothing and was just sentimental, how much more does he care about the things that are most precious?

We got a wrecker that took us all the way into the 76 gas station in Montgomery. Fixed our tire and got us home. We pulled in our driveway just in time to get the kids off to school.

All the way home I thanked God for all that he meant to me, all that he provided for us. I needed the miracle of the ring six months after I lost it, and he knew that. His timing is perfect.

Last-Minute Taxi

VONNY ALBERT

Several years ago, my husband and I were returning home from a Cubs game in Chicago. Traffic was tied up and on the way from the bus to the train, we got lost. We ended up in a neighborhood with a lot of abandoned factories with broken windows. We kept walking, having no idea where we were going. We seemed to be the only ones around, in the middle of a block with no traffic around us. Three men came toward us from the other side of the street. I felt very vulnerable because they were coming at us in an aggressive way. I began to pray like crazy. Just as the men approached, a taxi cab pulled up to us. We hadn't heard the cab coming. It seemed as though God just set it right next to us. The driver had pulled over to do some paperwork. We got in, and the driver got us to the train. It seems God comes through right when you need him to—right at the last minute sometimes.

I Can Pray No More

CHARLES PRICE JONES

One day as I staggered under the weight of ministry, I felt that I must be alone to talk with God about it. I locked myself in a room to reach out to the Lord with this matter. Oh the relief and help possible through prayer. It is good when burdened to pray it out; some phrase it "pray through." I prayed from about nine o'clock to about three o'clock. This was the burden of my prayer: "Lord, give me power to convince my people and my generation of the beauty of holiness and the advantages of righteousness." I saw that in God our salvation is both temporal and eternal. I desired that my people should see it. And so I prayed.

Between three and four o'clock in the afternoon I became exhausted. I lay down on the sofa by which I knelt and said, "Lord, I'm exhausted. I can pray no more." Then the Lord flooded me with blessing until, laughing and crying, I at last begged the Lord to desist. It seemed I could stand no more, my vision was clarified, my eyes were opened. I sensed God saying to me, "You shall write the hymns for your people." This he said six or seven times till it was fixed in my mind. I got up and went to the organ in the corner of the room, wrote a song titled "Praise the Lord," ruled off a tablet, set it to music, and sang it before I left the room.

The Meaning of Grace and Mercy

HELEN COPAN NEUBACHER

She lived with us for four years, my aunt—my mother's sister—until her death in November 1997. Those four years changed me forever.

My mother and her sister were as antipodal as silk and sand, day and night. As a young woman, my aunt had chosen a path that led her far from the road of faith that her family had traveled for generations. My mother chose the path of obedience and duty—obedience which was a gladness to her rather than a burden.

There are not many people who have been so prayed over, so anguished over, so wept over as my aunt had been. She came to live with my husband, children, and me because living alone had become frightening and impossible. We looked forward to surrounding her with love and watching her blossom. As time passed, however, she reciprocated clumsily and our attempts at communication became more and more garbled.

With all my heart I desired to be the faithful answer to the prayers of my deceased grandmother—and my still-praying mother—but I despaired of being able to love my aunt as I knew I should. When taking care of her became a round-the-clock commitment, I knew I was looking at the bottom of the barrel of my reserves, and I begged God not to let her die without her knowing how much I loved her and how much more he loved her.

Then God simply and graciously brought about a change in her. Her spirit of hardness, bitterness, melted away. The last weeks of her life became for her a contented kaleidoscope of timelessness and a hazy jumble of people and events—past and present. Even in the jumble of hospital time and the ever-changing staff of nurses, we had never seen her more at peace. In this dreamlike world of her new reality, she was able to shed old thorny barriers and feel and give love like a small child. She reached out to us and to God. And, at the end, God stepped into her life, picked her up, and took her Home.

Looking back, I see things much more clearly and I am thankful for a God who redeems lost time and lost lives, who answers a brokenhearted mother's prayer, and who, through this—the most difficult and richest experience of my life—taught me the meaning of grace and mercy.

Forty Years of Prayer

DON FIELDS

The conversion of my family took nearly forty years. The first conversion came when I was in the Navy and stole a Gideon Bible out of a hotel in Jacksonville, Florida, in 1951. I took the Bible back to the naval base and started reading it. Over the next three months I read the New Testament three times. The first time I read the Gospel of John, I thought, "If this book is right, then I am wrong." The third time I read John, I realized the truth of Jesus, but I did not have much of an idea of how someone could express their faith. I was not talking to anyone about this, just reading. One night the lights went off at ten o'clock, and I just cried out to God, "God, I know that I am a sinner and that the answer is in Jesus and what he's done. Please help me!" That is the point when I believed.

I prayed for my parents and my two brothers almost every day for the next couple of years while I was in the Navy. When I got out of the Navy I was so psyched up for my family to believe in Jesus that I went back and "dumped the truck" on them, and that produced a lot of tension. From that point on, I had to wait for clear opportunities to talk about Christianity.

Nine years after I stole that Bible, my father was heavily into drinking. He would often be gone for days at a time. During one of these times, my mother made a commitment to God. Assurance of her place in God's family was a very difficult thing for her to grasp, but gradually she gained a sense of security in her relationship with the Lord.

I had a bad relationship with my father, and he did not respond very well to discussions about faith. I realized that I had to work on my relationship with him to even have a right to be heard. I started going into the beer joints with him and waiting him out. This began to build a relationship between us that had not existed for many years. One night he called me and said he wanted to become a Christian. I said, "Dad, you are drunk." He said that he was but he would sober up if I would come to see him the next day. I did, and we talked for several hours. Three weeks later he declared his faith in Jesus. That was twenty-two years after my conversion.

Thirty-four years after I had become a believer, my next older brother, Bob, was diagnosed with cancer and had a brain tumor removed. I went to Evansville, Indiana, to see him in the hospital. He said, "Don, I want you to know that I am doing a lot of thinking about God." We started studying the Bible together by mail, and I visited him every few weeks. The cancer went fast. Bob became a believer only a few months before he died.

At the funeral, I said something about the conversations Bob and I had had before he died. After the funeral, my other brother, Philip, said to me, "Don, that was wonderful to hear about Bob and his becoming a Christian. I know you couldn't say those things about me, but it was great to hear them about Bob." Philip did not know it then, but a year and a half later he would also be diagnosed with a brain tumor.

During that year and a half, I took a trip with Philip to visit relatives in Wyoming. On the way back, we got into a conversation about spiritual things. He began studying a book on Christianity, and within the next year he became a believer.

For thirty-eight years I prayed for my family before they all came to Christ. Much of that time I would not have felt that there was much chance that they would become Christians, but I prayed for them and continued to talk to them about God. God is faithful and sure in doing his work in his own time.

Grace Notes

These grace notes
Decorate the darkness of today.
Like sparks they shine
Against the winter's lingering—
Pink tongues of peony
Pushing through damp earth,
And sparrows, freshly striped with white.
The sudden flocks of juncos come to feed.
Bold squirrels ride the branch tips
Till they bend and sway
To eat precariously of maple buds.
These give me hope
With promises that spring
Is riding in on this high wind.

ANNE KEITH

CHAPTER TWO

Simple Graces

Sometimes in the daily and the mundane,
God gives us signs of grace.

Miracle Cat

EMA-JEAN LLOYD

When I was ten, I owned a particularly special pet. Scout was a black and white cat, and unusually small for his two years, especially being an un-neutered tom. He was one of a trio of kittens that my family was given when I was eight, yet he and I had bonded immediately. He was undoubtedly *my* baby.

My cat was rarely home. It was a cat's heaven living next to an expanse of national forest land in Arizona. We soon grew used to his absences. He could be gone for days at a time, and then, all of a sudden, he would appear on the front step, howling to be let in.

Scout had been on one of these excursions when the accident occurred, so we hadn't missed him at all. Daddy found him in the shed, shivering with fear. He appeared to be bleeding from the nose, mouth, and ears. Mommy wrapped him up in a towel, and they were going to take him to be put to sleep at the vet's, but he clawed himself free and ran off. We didn't see him again for a week.

For some reason our whole family was conveniently gathered in the living room when he came back. We heard the familiar scratch as Scout scrabbled at the cat door in the back, and Mom went to see him. She shrieked; a small bundle of blood and matted fur crawled inside. The bleeding had stopped, but dried blood encrusted his face. Long cactus spines poked from his back, his throat had been slit, and his rib and hip bones jutted out from lack of food.

This time he wasn't afraid but rumbled his friendly steam-engine purr, glad to be back home. As Mom pulled out the cactus spines and tried to clean away some of the blood, all he did was purr and rub up against us. That night, Scout slept in *my* room, on *my* bed, rumbling the whole night.

The next morning, my parents decided again to take him on the one-way trip to the vet. Patching him up would cost too much. So they took him, Scout purring all the way.

I was absolutely devastated. Scout was a part of my family. How could my parents *do* this? Why, oh *why* did one of my best friends have to die? As I sobbed my young ten-year-old self to sleep that night, I sent up a prayer for myself and my baby.

In the morning, Mom called the vet's to be able to assure me that Scout was safe and out of pain.

Well, he was safe and out of pain, but still alive! Scout had purred, and loved, and trusted so completely that the vet just couldn't do it. Instead, he patched him up.

The vet told us how he had found a twenty-two bullet lodged in Scout's spine up in his neck. About half a dozen cactus spines were sunk into Scout's body, barely missing vital internal organs. He also said that it was probably a coyote that had attacked Scout, tearing his throat. The vet removed the bullet, extracted the cactus spines, stitched up Scout's throat, and, while my cat was still under anesthetic, neutered him. Scout was given a full course of antibiotics and confined under observation for the next two days and nights. Melanie, the assistant, assured my mother that she would love to keep my kitten. She was amazed that a cat would continue to purr in such pain. The only time he remained silent was when he was asleep.

I had mixed emotions about this information. Scout wasn't dead, I was joyful for that, but now *he couldn't be my baby anymore.* Then I was told that he could be. My parents were offered a reduced price of fifty dollars for his patchwork and neutering. So, God spared both my cat and my already bruised emotions. Call it what you like. I call it a miracle.

Soap, Toothpaste, and a Pair of Shoes

ELS MAAGDENBERG

Hundreds of hippies and dropouts were swarming the Mediterranean beaches, and I was one of them. A young girl with little money in search of a small job to keep me going, I came in contact with some believers in Israel's most southern town. Hearing the words of Jesus and seeing the joy in their eyes made me reach out for him, and I was invited to spend some time with my new faith-friends, living in a hostel.

I hadn't felt cared for in the preceding years, so it made some impression when they explained to me that Jesus not only saved, but also cared. How would he show he cared?

I still had very little money, but life's expenses go on! A woman needs to wash and brush teeth and walk in shoes. I was running out of these happy little necessities, and I can't remember if I actually prayed. I imagine it was more like a small worry on my mind. But one morning, a man who had been visiting from Holland walked over to my room and said, with a shy smile: "I work in a soap factory, and I brought some samples to give away. I would like you to have one." He handed me a bright blue bar of soap.

Within a few days, upon walking home, I found a brand-new tube of toothpaste lying in the dusty, dry gutter. I was elated. To me, this was God's way of telling me that he was aware of my every need.

A few days later, walking on the street with a friend, we found a pair of sneakers in the bushes. They weren't new and were a size or two too big, but I loved them and had them for months afterward. My God wasn't only big enough to save my soul, but he was also near enough to care for me.

Airport Angel

REBECCA PUNTIGAM

"Well, young man, I see you have your boarding pass, but where is your ticket? I can't give you a seat assignment or let you on the plane without it." The passenger agent pensively eyed my fourteen-year-old son, Joel, and then looked over at me.

I moved up to the counter with my five-year-old daughter, Marissa, and my sixteen-year-old autistic son, Nathan. I hoped I could straighten out the problem with Joel's ticket quickly, but the tense situation became the catalyst to set Nate off into an uncontrollable temper tantrum. As he began to scream and dart away, I had to shift all my attention to him, pulling him down onto the terminal floor where he could not knock anyone or anything over. All I could do was look hopelessly at the agent, leaving Joel's first solo plane trip in question.

The agent came over to talk to me further. Seeing I could be of no help right then, she suddenly announced that although the ticket was missing, surely Joel had checked in properly because he had his baggage claim checks. Therefore, he could get on the plane. I was too busy to do more than quickly thank her and nod good-bye to Joel.

I concentrated on trying to get Nate calm enough to let him stand up so we could successfully leave the airport terminal and get to our car. People walked around us giving us puzzled or concerned glances. A passerby offered Nate some corn chips. Nate flung them away and continued thrashing his arms and legs. Another adult stopped and helped hold Nate down for a few moments before he apologetically left to catch his plane. In the past, when Nate had gotten out of control in public, there had always been my husband, older children, or another adult I knew who could help remove Nate to a place where he could calm down. I now felt completely helpless and had no idea what I could do by myself.

This was just the sort of situation I had always dreaded happening. For several years, I had not gone out in public with just Nathan and Marissa. Nate's behavior was too unpredictable, and Marissa was too young to care for herself if Nate ran off. Yet, here we were alone.

This had not been the original plan, of course. After I had gotten the nonrefundable tickets, my husband realized that Joel's departure time conflicted with a seminar he had promised to give. Clark was not able to come to the airport, but we had prayed for God's help and protection while I would be responsible for the children by myself.

There I was, crouched on the floor, holding Nathan down, while Marissa sat beside me with an ashen face. Suddenly a man appeared at my side. He was extremely calm and seemed totally knowledgeable about how to handle my situation. He took over with Nate, announcing that he was a fireman and had a mentally challenged brother.

He quickly managed to get Nate upright and moving towards the escalator and the airport subway. I followed with my frightened little girl clinging to my hand. We steadily moved out of the terminal into the parking garage. Although we talked very little, the stranger revealed that this was his first time at Seattle International Airport.

Finally Nathan was safely inside the car, though he was wildly kicking everything in sight. The stranger expressed concern over whether I could yet handle my son. I thanked him for his help and assured him that Nate would soon calm down. Marissa and I quickly got into the car. She immediately threw up her breakfast in response to the morning's events. I momentarily forgot the helpful stranger as I cleaned up the mess and drove away.

The phone was ringing when we walked through the house door. It was the passenger agent calling to see how we were. She told us that she could see how worried Joel was at leaving his family at such an upsetting moment, so she had upgraded his seat from coach to first class, where he sat beside another teenage boy. Having a son herself, she knew Joel needed something fun and different to occupy his mind. That serendipity succeeded! Joel was full of his exciting plane experience when he called several hours later, laughing that his brother's disability sometimes brought good surprises.

Since that summer morning, I have repeatedly reflected on how we were given help to get out of a difficult set of circumstances. God gave us a trusting airline agent who took care of Joel and gave him a better trip than he might have had otherwise. The stranger arrived to help us just when the situation seemed hopeless. Why didn't he have any time restraints? Was he a man whom God had placed just where his special skills were needed? Or was he an angel? I do not know the answer to that question. I do know without a doubt that the Lord protected and rescued us when we were in trouble, just as he promises.

Grace Underground*

JO KADLECEK

I had just moved to New York City when I first started thinking about this strange notion of grace. I couldn't help but notice it all around me: riding beside me on the subways, walking in front of me on the busy streets, staring past me in the book stores, cafés, museums, and theaters that comprise this sleepless place.

To get to Washington Heights, my neighborhood, you have to take the $1.50 subway, the "A" train to be exact, which lets you out about a hundred feet from the street.

Directly down, that is.

Underneath the park.

You wander out of the subway, up a grungy flight of stairs, to an elevator where you wait several minutes while it delivers passengers between Washington Heights/Fort Tryon and New York's eerie underworld of transportation.

Every time I came home on the subway from a meeting in mid-Manhattan thirty minutes or so away, climbing up the steps, waiting for the elevator, I noticed the same thing: The city had paid some willing soul real money to sit inside that moving metal box and carry us from the ground to Fort Washington Street or vice versa. All day long, he sat there, waiting for the elevator to fill up with busy people, pressing a button, and riding through the earth for two or three minutes. When it would stop, he'd push another button, watch the people exit, wait for a new group to enter, and then ride back through the earth for two or three minutes to start over again. An eight-hour shift of button-pushing with no sunlight or fresh air or variation, except in the bodies that crowded his eight by ten space, and even they must have begun to look the same.

I could think of no worse job in the universe than to be a subway-elevator man in the most populated city in the country.

But even bad jobs have good moments. One evening I joined a group of well-dressed professionals as we crowded into the box after a long subway trip. Shoulder to shoulder we stood, waiting for the routine ride to end. I looked at the weary faces of business women and Wall Street men. I noticed the brown glossy eyes of the elevator man, whose peppered white hair posed a stark contrast to his weathered brown face. Wrinkles sagged beneath his eyes, crowding out once-firm smile lines. I wondered if anything in his day had made him smile, but tired myself from a full day, I looked away at the elevator numbers. And I waited.

Then an elegant small woman with perfect gray hair and powdered-white skin wearing a blue suit asked the elevator man how his day had gone. He grunted something about cold drafts and obnoxious kids and cranky managers. She nodded her perfect head, as if she, too, had experienced the same frustrations all day. Then a Wall Street man entered the conversation, wondering if the elder city worker had seen the Knicks' game the night before. Another asked about the weather. Like old friends, they shared life for two or three minutes until life ended and a door opened. And as it did, one by one the professionals exited and dropped a simple "Thank you!" in the direction of the tired elevator man who smiled and nodded in return. "See ya tomorrow," he grunted.

The exchange of dignity suddenly awarded him the most important job of the day. And I marveled at the redemptive story I had just witnessed, one that settled in for me like a good bedtime tale. I shook my head in wonder as the crowd carried me out of the box with them. How could tired human hearts still manage to be kind to one another at the end of a long, hard day? How could total strangers who shared nothing but a ride through the earth act as if they'd been friends all their lives? How could people in a city full of millions of other bodies crowded into a tiny island called Manhattan manage any sort of civility toward each other at all?!

Some say God has abandoned our evil, bent world. I say, maybe they haven't been to New York City.

Winter Chestnut

LUCI SHAW

It was late autumn in Vancouver, a hiatus of chilling rain—the year too far gone for warmth and golden days, too early for Christmas.

I left a friend's house after a very early-morning Great Books discussion group, descended the wooden steps, and moved along the walk toward my car. Under my feet the concrete sidewalk felt mushy. Looking down, I realized that it was so thickly carpeted with wide, yellow chestnut leaves that the pavement was completely covered. The parent chestnut tree loomed above me, muddy gold in the early gray of the rain-filled dawn. A long day of reading, tutorials, and teaching lay before me. I was already tired. It was cold. I shivered.

Then, I felt as much as heard a faint plop behind me. As I turned and looked back, the green, spiny husk of the chestnut that had just thudded on the leaves split open, and the glossy, brown nucellus rolled toward me, as if heaven had not only dropped me a gift but had unwrapped it to save me the trouble.

I love chestnuts, the silk feel of them, their pregnant weight, their uneven roundness, their satin shine. This one seemed to gleam with potential life at a time of year when everything else was dying or rotting or going to sleep. I picked up the small present and put it in my raincoat pocket. My day had been renewed.

In time my chestnut lost some of its plump gloss, but it stayed in my pocket all winter. Every time I fingered it I was warmed by the thought of its Giver and the timing of the gift.

One Explosive Sneeze

MARGARET JENSEN

When my younger brother Gordon was scheduled for nasal surgery to correct difficult breathing, the thought of the operation made me shudder. I had undergone my own surgery at home in Winnipeg. I had helped spread a blanket on the table, then listened to Papa's instruction about the use of the can of chloroform in his hand. The next thing I had known was Papa's white face and my sore throat. Good-bye tonsils! That was in our kitchen, but now Gordon was going to the hospital!

As we gathered for prayer, Mama again reminded God of his promises, that if we ask anything in his name, it shall be done. "We ask that the source of this problem be removed . . . and bless the doctor and the nurses," she finished.

In the next few minutes mischievous Gordon managed to get a pepper can open, and one explosive sneeze sent a button, lodged in his nasal passage, flying across the room.

Mama made sure we learned the lesson of the day: "'My God shall supply all your need,' and today, children, God supplied surgery through a pepper can."

"You Can't Bother God with Something Like That"

VONNY ALBERT

When my aunt died, I drove my family from the Chicago area to Indiana for the funeral. It was January, with the typical midwestern cold and snow. I had been close to my aunt and was dreading the funeral as well as the drive. She had died suddenly and relatively young. The gray sky and freezing conditions did not make me feel better.

The drive proved to be as bad as I had feared. I could barely see the road through the dirt and grime on the windshield. Then the windshield wiper fluid froze. I felt as though I was peering through barely pulled-back curtains. I wondered again why I had to be the one driving and why we had a funeral to go to in the first place.

Exasperated, I prayed aloud, "Lord, just let this windshield clear." Another person in the car responded, "Oh, Vonny, you can't bother God with something like that." My heart sank, but I went on praying.

As we continued driving and the windshield still didn't clear, I wondered if maybe she was right. Why would God care about such a small thing as my windshield? Then, just as I was about to give up, I tried the wiper fluid again. This time it worked! The dirt of the trip fell away, opening those curtains I hadn't been able to see through. I looked at the others in the car and asked, "Now who do we thank for this?"

The windshield stayed clear the rest of the trip. On a dreary and grief-filled day, God provided a reminder that he will provide for us in every way we need him to—even in things "too small to bother God with."

Quieting the Storm

CHRISTINE HILGER

In springtime in Texas, thunderstorms with lightning bolts shook the ground, raindrops as wide as silver dollars pounded the hot pavement until puddles formed and currents flowed. It was a time when dinner was often interrupted by the sound of the town's tornado sirens, and the look of adventuresome delight crossed both of my brothers' faces as they raced outside for a look.

The drill was always the same. If we were on the dry side of the storm, my oldest brother would prop a rickety ladder against the side of the house and hold it while my other brother and sometimes my sister, or any of the neighborhood kids who happened to be at our house at the time, scurried to the roof. I was too little to climb ladders, so I stood below listening to the oohs and ahhs of my siblings until my mother, tipped by a neighbor who spent most of her day keeping track of the comings and goings of the neighborhood, came out the back door scolding at the top of her lungs for everyone to get back inside.

The years passed and finally the spring came when I was old enough to climb the ladder. It was a dry spring, and I was beginning to think I would end up waiting another year, when it happened. The siren sounded. The older children charged out of the house with me following as closely as I could.

The wood shingles creaked as I walked to the southwest portion of the roof. I didn't know what to expect, what could possibly be so mesmerizing as to halt arguments in mid-sentence and bring otherwise squabbling siblings to such unity.

I looked into the distance and there it was, a rotating wall cloud. The funnel never touched the ground. Instead, it simply dipped and danced as the thunder rumbled and the rain approached. I held my sister's hand and watched. It was beyond description. The power contained in the storm was tangible. I could see it, hear it, taste the dust it was blowing into my face. And at that moment I knew terror, for although my sister reminded me of how Jesus quieted the storm when he and his disciples were at sea, I secretly believed that I was looking into something more powerful than God himself.

The years passed. Springs came and sirens sounded, but I never followed the others to the roof again. Then, one day in early May during my junior year in high school, the weather turned ominous. I was sitting in the library with my English class, putting the final touches on a term paper when the sky turned noticeably dark.

I looked out the library window. Cars put on their headlights as if the sun had been completely blotted out of the sky. A few moments passed as students gathered near the windows, then a curtain of green light spread across the campus.

A nervous young man called out, “Auntie Em! Auntie Em!” as the intercom squawked signaling that we were about to hear from our reclusive principal. His words were firm and clear. We were to get out into the hallway immediately and assume emergency positions.

The sound of scuffling steps and large hailstones crashing onto the roof filled the library, but instead of feeling terror, I felt a sense of God’s peace cover me like a blanket. Its power was all around me. It was tangible and real. With inner eyes I could see it cloaking me in protection. With inner ears I could hear it telling me that all was well.

The storm did not miraculously dissipate, and some things were damaged, including my ancient car that was generously pelted by hailstones. But the storm passed, taking with it my doubt. One of my brothers now chases storms in a car, and I join him from time to time. For my brother, and for me, there is no greater thrill than standing before such power knowing that it is as if it were nothing when compared to the One who holds us in the palm of his hand.

Belonging

CHERYL DONALDSON

Often when I stayed with my grandfather while I was growing up, I would look into his room in the morning and see him by his bed praying. Later in the day, he would tell me, "Cheryl, I talked to the Lord about you today," or, "I prayed for you by name today." He wore out the knees of his pajamas because he prayed in the morning so much.

My grandfather always started his prayers with, "Father, we thank Thee that we belong to Thee." Growing up, I didn't appreciate how significant his prayers were. But I liked that idea of belonging—"We belong to Thee."

When my cousin got married recently, my family celebrated my grandfather's ninety-fifth birthday. As we were discussing our grandfather's impact on us, each person seemed to have the same story:

"I remember seeing Granddad praying by his bed in the morning," or, "Grandad always tells me that he prays for me by name."

At the end of my cousin's wedding ceremony, Grandad got up to pray. With gentleness and humility, he bowed his head in front of his growing and changing family and began: "Father, we thank Thee that we belong to Thee. . . ."

My grandfather's prayers are signs of God's grace to me and to my extended family. For thirty-one years I've heard those prayers. And when I hear those prayers mentioning my name I know that not only does my granddad take joy in the fact that he belongs to God, I take joy in the fact that my granddad belongs to me.

A Curious Guardian Angel

BARBARA MCKINNEY

One pleasant winter afternoon in Chicago, I had to go to a paint/wallpaper store across town by public transportation. Before I left, my husband prayed with me for protection. He couldn't go across town with me, but he walked me to the bus stop, waited for me to board, and I was on my way.

I reached my stop, alighted from the bus, and crossed Stony Island Avenue to the store. Upon approaching the paint store, I saw there, rounding the corner, the largest, reddest, most muscular Doberman pinscher I have ever seen. Even this dog's face seemed to have muscles. I thought, *Oh God, help.*

As I entered the store, there were other patrons exiting the store, but upon spotting the dog, they quickly went back inside. They stood looking out of the window, waiting for the dog to leave. Several other patrons saw this little group looking out the window and one man pointed to the dog and explained the reason for the delay.

All the while, I continued to shop for the items I had come for, believing that the dog would be gone by the time I finished. I finished my shopping and headed for the cash register. While paying for the items, I heard someone say, "He's gone."

Someone else said, "Great! Let me hurry up and get to my car."

Good! I thought, as I paid for my items. The gentleman bagged them, and I proceeded to the exit door. As soon as I exited the store and stepped out to cross the street, the dog came back around the corner. I said, "Oh God," and at that moment a peace came over me. I was not afraid.

Together the dog and I crossed the avenue to the bus stop. The bus was not coming, so, as usual, I began to walk toward the next stop. The dog walked with me. When we reached the next bus stop, I went up to the curb to look for the bus. While I was looking for the bus, the dog stood by the pole at the bus stop and waited for me. I did not see the bus and continued to walk. The dog continued to walk with me. At each bus stop, we repeated the same actions: I would look for the bus, and the dog would stop and wait for me. As we walked, he never left my side.

While progressing to one of the loneliest bus stops, I noticed that two large men were walking aggressively toward me. As we got closer, though, the two men left the sidewalk and began walking in the middle of the street (presumably intimidated by my companion). They called to me, "Hey, miss, is that your dog?!" I just smiled and kept walking.

Finally, we reached 93rd Street, where I was going to change buses. By this time, school had let out and children were on their way home. Many of the children were afraid of the dog. I told them not to run and that he would not bother them. Fortunately, they believed me and went about what they were doing. The dog and I, along with some other people, stood at the bus stop and waited. Then the bus came. I boarded. And the big red muscular dog left.

I have been in that area many times since, but have never seen that dog again. That dog, I believe, was my guardian angel for that time. He never left my side, he never barked at anything or anyone. Nothing distracted him. His attention was always on me. Who knows what those two men would have done had I been alone? But I was protected. I thank and praise God for the vigilant watchfulness of that big dog.

Mystery

There is a winged shape,
Elusive as a spark.
Stretching to catch it
With the mind,
The world goes dark.
But holding peace,
Hands quiet
In one place,
All motions cease
And spirit feels
The breath of angels' wings.

ANNE KEITH

CHAPTER THREE

God's Mysterious Grace

Sometimes the biggest mystery of grace is that God keeps extending it to us.

The Answer

LINDA WASHINGTON

Once more I felt angry at God.

To those who know me, that comes as no surprise. During that season of my life, impatience over not receiving an answer to prayer, a bout of unemployment, financial loss, disappointment, and doubt all added up to anger—anger in the worst way.

Oh, I knew the drill. God's answers to prayer are yes, no, and wait. You have to be persistent in prayer. I knew that. I had been a Christian most of my life—ever since I was a kid. But emotional pain doesn't always listen to reason.

One November day, Election Day to be exact, I told myself that I would no longer pray. *Why should I pray if God doesn't answer?* I reasoned. *Obviously, he doesn't care.*

I set out for the polling place that morning just before 6 A.M. The doors had not officially opened as yet. While I waited, a man came in. If I had to describe him today, I couldn't, nor could I then. I had a vague sense of height and horn-rimmed glasses. He smiled and said hello. I was barely in a mood to be civil. I grunted something that sounded vaguely like "Hello."

The man suddenly said, "Are you saved?"

That merited him a look. "Yes," I reluctantly replied. I couldn't help feeling guilty, having decided to stop communicating with God.

"Do you think God doesn't hear your prayers?"

I contemplated him in stunned silence. *How could he know this?* "Sometimes," I replied.

"Well, God's got big ears."

The conversation ended then, as the doors to the polling place were suddenly opened. I lost sight of the man after that. But I never forgot what he told me—or that God had used a stranger to touch my life that day.

A Special Kind of Christmas Eve

DON BOOTH

Even though I was almost twenty-four and had been in the Navy and flying around the South China Sea in World War II for a couple of years, the other four men in our crew on the South Buffalo Railway called me "Kid."

I was on the "extra" board, which meant I was called to come in to work the shift on Christmas Eve afternoon on a crew that worked behind the Bethlehem Steel strip mill. When I reported to the little dingy yard shanty, I noticed two burlap bags and some paper grocery bags. I knew what that probably meant. We'd work until seven o'clock and then we'd put the engine away and "party." Alcohol was one of railroaders' worst occupational hazards.

As expected, at seven o'clock my crew put our engine into one of the mills, and we headed out into the black of night with only the feeble light from the switchman's lamps to guide us through the knee-deep snow. The moon was full and the snow glistened like a pile of diamonds. It was a glorious reminder of what Christmas Eve was really all about. And I was carrying a cold, wet, rattling burlap bag.

We reached a ramshackle old house with broken front steps and a sagging porch. The three kids that flew out to greet us made us feel like special guests. Obviously, these men visited them often during lunch breaks bearing "gifts." We entered the kitchen and the table was all set. A familiar smell and the diffused light reminded me of my grandmother's kitchen—kerosene lamps and a wood-burning cook stove.

I looked around the ring of excited people and was introduced to a tiny, eighty-year-old grandma, as well as the mom who looked terribly tired, Uncle Clarence who had a distinctive, long sharp nose and limped from an immobile knee, a pretty teenage girl in tattered clothes, a pair of rambunctious fourteen-year-old twins, and a tiny four-year-old named Nellie who was everybody's favorite.

We sat wherever we could find anything that looked like it would hold us. Around us were several wooden packing boxes stenciled with the name "Bethlehem," several chairs with springs that had long ago given up trying, a piano bench pulled up to a tired-looking old upright piano missing most of its ivories, and a scraggly looking Christmas tree that looked like a cast-off from someone's garden, trimmed in strips of colored paper pasted into a chain.

In the corner, a weary old stove burned coal that looked suspiciously like the coal in the pile over behind the railroad yard shanty. We took off our heavy coats and the kids put several of them on and admired how warm they were. I saw their coats on the rack by the kitchen stove and felt a little guilty for having my fleece jacket.

At the family's insistence we sat down at the table to a mixture of all kinds of dishes—canning jars for glasses and plastic picnic knives and forks.

Grandma said that Rosie, the teenager, would say grace, and I saw a miracle: Boomer, our conductor who always wore a railroad cap rain or shine, took his hat off. His head was as bald as an egg, but, for a few minutes, he didn't care.

The twins eyed the meat—fried rabbit—eagerly. Mom gave a subdued reminder that they were to take tiny portions because they wanted to treat their visitors politely. I could hardly eat anything. I noticed the other fellas sighed and said they weren't too hungry, either. Big lunch, you know. The twins were glad to clean it up.

After we ate supper and did the dishes, the fellas took out what was in the other bags. There was a shawl for grandma, a Bible for mom, a nice tie for Uncle Clarence who was a salesman, and a couple of games for the twins. A nice pair of boots for Rosie and a really warm snowsuit for Nellie. The fellas had mittens and hats for each of them that their wives had knitted. It was a great time.

Then, it was time for our "program." Grandma said we'd all have to do something to entertain the rest. She whistled "The Old Rugged Cross." Mom passed around a homemade cookie to each person. Teenage Rosie played a couple of songs on the piano and was very good, even if a couple of strings were broken. The twins performed a couple of funny skits they'd seen at the Boy Scouts, and Nellie recited a poem she'd learned in Sunday school. Uncle Clarence did a couple of old bar tricks with some peanuts and safety matches and soda straws.

Then it was our turn. Boomer took out a harmonica and played several Civil War songs. Jerry took out a couple of old grocery bags we'd brought and a crayon from his pocket and drew some remarkably good caricatures of each member of the family. Larry O'Shea sang in an Irish tenor style that surprised us all. Sparky did some card tricks.

Then, they all looked at me. "It's your turn, Kid," they laughed.

"Well, I learned a Christmas story for our church camp, if that's okay," I said.

"What's it about?" one of the twins asked.

"It was written a long time ago by a man named Henry VanDyke. It's about a fella named Artaban, who was a Magi like the kings in the regular story. But Artaban never made it to Jesus because he got slowed down helping some people and he missed going along. It's called 'The Other Wise Man.'"

Once I got the first couple of words out, I just rode along on a wave of inspiration. I haven't had such freedom or such an appreciative audience since. I've never told it as well as I did that night. After I finished, it was several minutes before anyone said anything.

We got our hats and coats on and headed back toward the plant and the bright lights. When we got back up in our engine and the fellas were busy opening the door and lining up the switches, Sparky scratched his ear, rubbed his chin and chuckled as he punched me on the arm, "You're okay, Kid." There were tears in his eyes. Among railroad men, that's a high compliment.

About eleven years went by. I had gotten a parking ticket in South Buffalo, and I was headed for the town hall. A thin fella in his late sixties, a little bent over and with a distinctive sharp, hooked nose, crossed the street and entered a restaurant. He had one stiff leg. I knew him but couldn't place him.

It was Uncle Clarence.

I entered the restaurant as he was opening his paper and it all came back to me—the kerosene lamps, the scraggly tree, the stove, the Bethlehem Steel coal, the supper that was more than a family could afford for some people they cared about, and the kids. Oh, yes, the kids.

I slid into the booth across from the thin-faced man with the sharp nose and said, "Merry Christmas, Uncle Clarence," and stuck out my hand. It was July and about ninety degrees outside.

"Merry Christmas?" he muttered, a little testily, wondering who I was. He squinted, looked a little closer, and snapped his fingers as his face broke out in the lopsided smile I remembered. "You're that kid who told the story about the Other Wise Man at our party that night." He grabbed my hand and shook it in a way that made everyone in the restaurant turn to look.

I asked where everyone was after all this time.

Grandma hadn't lived through the winter. Mom had moved to West Virginia to live with a sister. Rosie had become a missionary and was working in Alaska. One of the twins had died of rheumatic fever, the other was a stock car driver in California, and Nellie was a school teacher.

"They tore that whole neighborhood down to enlarge the strip mill, and we had to move, but we spoke of that Christmas Eve party many times," Uncle Clarence sighed. A big tear ran down his cheek.

I nodded but no words would come out. For a few minutes, I thought I could smell kerosene lamps, a scraggly Christmas tree, and the wet clothes of some scruffy old railroad men. I remembered the eyes of a boy seeing the story of the Other Wise Man in the fire of some South Buffalo Railway coal.

We toasted our memory of the party with our coffee and agreed it had been a very special gift in time.

Train Friend*

JODI SCHROEDER

At one point during my three-year stay in the Czech Republic, I had to travel alone from Slovakia to Kosice. Although I would have to change trains once and then find the airline office in the city to catch a shuttle to the airport, I was only slightly anxious about the trip. I felt more comfortable with the language, and I looked forward to returning to my Czech home.

After about an hour-long train ride, winding through picturesque mountains and valleys, we arrived at Presov, where I would change trains to go to Kosice. I checked the board and noticed that a track number for Kosice was not yet assigned. As it was still early, I was not worried and went up to the platform to read my book. Every few minutes I glanced toward the board for the platform number.

Soon it was less than five minutes before the train was supposed to leave, and still there was no number. A young girl came up to me and started speaking very quickly. I only picked up the word Kosice so I pointed to myself and said "Kosice" also. She rattled on and then left to find a conductor. I went back to my book.

It was only about a moment later that she ran to me and grabbed my hand, and together we began running away from the station. Where was she going? She kept pulling me faster than my reluctant feet wanted to go. We were headed toward a bus, and she gripped my hand more firmly as she squeezed through the crowds. She jumped on the bus and saved me a seat. I only remember the extent of her smile as I sat down next to her. She looked so pleased with herself.

Meanwhile, I just sat there and wondered what was going on and if I would ever make my flight and why I was on a bus. The bus pulled away and after about twenty minutes, I glanced out the window and noticed some construction workers stationed on the railroad tracks. It finally dawned on me that they were repairing the tracks and that this was why the bus was necessary. Sure enough, just beyond the construction, the bus pulled into a small station where a train waited for us. Once again, my "friend" grabbed my hand and got us both seats. She continued to grin and I became more and more amazed. What an impact it made on me to think that such a great and powerful God cares enough to help a naive missionary girl catch a train.

A Bit of Heavenly Wisdom

LILIAS TROTTER

One of the girls in the village, that little pickle Melha, went right up to her nearly blind father and pointed to one of the pictures on the wall—of the Lord calling a little child to him—and said, "Look at Jesus."

"I have no eyes O my daughter—I cannot see," was the answer. The baby lifted her head and eyes to the picture and said, "O Jesus, look at father!" —Was not that a bit of heavenly wisdom?

Answered Prayers and Divine Graces

JANET CALLENDER

When my father died of a massive heart attack, our family grieved deeply because of the suddenness of his death when he was seemingly so healthy. But looking back, I can see the hand of God in many of the answered prayers and divine graces that surrounded his death. Like the conversation he and Mom had the night before he died.

In this conversation they talked about Dad's secretary. Dad had had a secretary who was a single mom. He had spent time with her and done nice things for her, like fixing stuff around the house and dropping by with food when she or her son was sick. Mom had always wondered about this relationship, never feeling completely comfortable with it but never able to come right out and ask about it. She would have wondered forever if not for that last talk.

By God's grace, they talked about that secretary that night. "Nothing ever happened," Dad said just before bed. And he went on to explain to Mom how he felt responsible for that woman and her son, how he felt that they needed a lot of encouragement and support because of the difficulties of single parenting and of growing up without a father's constant presence.

Did he somehow know what would happen? Mom clung to that conversation afterward. At the funeral, when the secretary came to pay her respects, Mom could graciously and securely listen to her tell of all the kind things Dad had done for her and her son.

Another sign of grace involved my sister. Long before my father died, my sister's marriage had fallen apart, and in her hurt she had started doubting her faith. Then she was in a major car accident, her house flooded, and she became ill with a debilitating, chronic illness. Church people abandoned her, and our family was hundreds of miles away. She was unable to work full-time and had huge debts. She stopped going to church, and her sons began to experiment with drugs. She and her sons barely made it to the funeral, as she was really too ill for such a long drive. But she did make it.

Some weeks after the funeral, my sister shared something very special. I talked with her about the sense I had of Dad's presence. Since his death he had seemed very close. My sister felt the same presence. "Jesus has seemed very far away the last few years," she said, "but since Dad died Dad seems very close, and he's sending me Jesus' love."

During that time also, a blanket of debt and financial worries covered the siblings. My sister owed thousands of dollars in medical bills. My brother's sales job had dropped off, and he and his wife struggled to pay for their children's schooling. My husband had lost his job and was working out of the house, and my income was not enough to support the family. We had all been praying for a financial break. Then my mother shocked us. She renounced the estate and passed my father's assets directly to us. My brother was filled with gratitude. My husband and I with thankful hearts paid off the debts we had accrued. And I listened to my sister weep on the phone as she began to grasp the meaning of our mother's action. "You can pay off all your bills and put a down payment on a condo," I told her.

"My medical bills are thousands of dollars. I'm so far in debt I should declare bankruptcy."

"But you'll be able to pay it all off," I said.

"How could I do that?" she asked, beginning to sob.

"I've seen the bank statements. I know how much you'll receive. You can pay off all those bills and be able to receive a small income," I told her.

The phone was silent except for her low crying. "I had no idea," she whispered into the phone.

Finally, I will never forget Easter that year. My dad's presence had seemed very distinct and close since his death. His presence seemed loving and affirming. It was a deep comfort in the grief. But I also had a sense that it was Jesus' presence, not my father's, on which I should be focusing. On Easter I struggled with this, envisioning Jesus on the cross and my father between us. "I must go," my father said. Like Jesus ascending to heaven, Dad had to move on. "Look to the cross," he told me.

We were singing "How Great Thou Art," a hymn we'd sung at the funeral. I couldn't stop weeping as I felt my father's presence pulling away. I knew I had to turn my eyes on Jesus, and maybe Dad knew that, too.

Prayer through the Night

VINITA HAMPTON WRIGHT

My father died after years of dealing with diabetes. His last couple of years were with much suffering spent in and out of the hospital. Months after he died, my mother told me this story:

There was one night when I came home from the hospital and I knew—for the first time—that he was never coming home again. It was the saddest night of my life. I'd had a lot of trouble sleeping and was afraid I wouldn't sleep at all that night because I was so upset. But I went right to sleep, slept all night, then woke up with a peace I had never experienced before through all of this. I found out later that the church had had a prayer chain going all night for me.

Road Trip

LINDA WASHINGTON

My parents, Preston and Susie, love to travel. Of all their adventures, there is one that none of us will ever forget.

While driving to Wichita, Kansas, during their vacation one summer, Dad said to Mom, "Let's pull over and see how far we are from Salina." (At Salina they would leave Highway 70 to change to Highway 135.) At a truck stop, Dad noticed a man whose truck had broken down. The man asked Dad for a ride to Salina.

Mom was wary about picking up a stranger. After a quick word of prayer, she mentioned having a sense that God had something for my parents to do.

On the way to Salina, the man related the sad story of how he had been present at a public pool two days previously when a little girl drowned. Mom and Dad listened sympathetically. Soon after that, they dropped the man off at his house. Days later, they went on to Colorado. They had decided to take a backroad south of Colorado Springs. On their way, they noticed the same van everywhere they stopped. After pausing on a mountainside to view the sunset, they struck up a conversation with the people in the van—the Pedersons (not their real name). They were a couple from Salina, Kansas, on their way to California. They mentioned how they grieved the loss of their daughter—the very same one Mom and Dad's passenger had seen drown. The Pedersons didn't know who the man was, nor did they remember seeing him before.

Mom and Dad were an answer to prayer for that grieving couple. They were able to administer God's love to them. Yet had they not picked up the man at the truck stop, they would have missed an opportunity to be a blessing to someone else.

Joy in the Morning

ALLISON JOHNSON

Six months after I was diagnosed with leukemia, I had to have a bone marrow transplant. By this time, my husband, Rod, and I were getting used to my long stays at the hospital. Rod usually did not stay with me overnight because the sleeper-chair in the room was too uncomfortable to sleep in, and he needed to care for our two-year-old son at home. One morning, however, about a week and a half after the transplant, Rod felt a strong urging to stay with me that night. Looking back, it seems this was a prompting from God.

Rod came to the hospital that afternoon while my mom stayed with our son. It was such a treat having Rod there, knowing he would be there all night. He read to me as I rested.

While he was reading, I grew increasingly uncomfortable physically. I'd been feeling miserable all the time anyway, so I tried to ignore the discomfort. The nurse I had that day wasn't very responsive, and I didn't want to bother her with what was probably normal.

Rod, however, could tell I was having problems breathing. He grew concerned and called the nurse. When the nurse didn't respond immediately, Rod went to get someone else to help. He insisted something was wrong and told the nurses they had to do something about it. All this time I was overwhelmed but didn't know what to do.

Finally Rod got someone to look at me. Soon medical personnel filled my room. It turned out I was having congestive heart failure—my heart had been damaged from the chemotherapy treatments. Nurses hooked me up to a breathing machine. Rod and the hospital staff made sure I stayed awake all night so my heart would stay healthy. The next day I was moved to intensive care, where I stayed until my heart recovered.

If I had been alone that night, I probably would not have told anybody I was feeling uncomfortable. By the time I realized what was happening, I might have been too hazy to ask for help. Because Rod was there, I got on the breathing machine in good time. Rod was also able to call our parents, and he asked his brother and our pastor to come pray with us.

During that scary night, I held on to the verse from Psalms, "Joy comes in the morning," so tightly it was as if it was in my hand. It gave me something to hope for.

We found out later that the pastor's wife had called others in the church, and they had a prayer chain going for me through the night. In the morning, two women from church came to be with me so Rod could get some rest.

God's care through Rod's presence with me, and the prayers of the people Rod called, got me from night to morning. I had many months of physical and emotional pain after that. But through that incident, God reminded us that he was caring for us. Rod and I went through a scary, dark night, yet as we look back, we see God's faithfulness to us and remember that mornings of joy did come.

Car Ride

CHRIS WAVE WITH KIM BOLTON

The old woman's gloveless hands clutched the grocery cart as she steered into the icy wind. The cart wobbled and stalled crossing the rails of the empty train tracks. Snow fell in thick chunks blotting out the afternoon sun. She was a painful sight against the inclemency of the day.

Oblivious to the angry honkings of speeding cars, she pushed her cart straight into the heart of traffic, aiming for a thin median dividing the lanes. The median tapered to nothing in less than a hundred feet. It had all the earmarks of a suicide mission.

I didn't really have time to help her. I was already late for the carpool pick up. But the image of her peril refused to let me pass on.

"I'd like to give you a ride," I called as I pulled alongside her. Angry commuters protested the delay with screeching tires and blaring horns. The old woman said nothing. “Please get in. I’ll load your groceries.” Still, she said nothing. Her eyes, piercing and nervous, conveyed no hint of understanding. Her gaze darted suspiciously all around but never once met my eyes.

Coming to a stop ahead of her, I slid the van door open. She grasped the seat back, her hands turned whitish with the struggle to pull herself in. Most of the fingers on her right hand ended after the first joint. Thick scars covered the stubs like band-aids made of flesh.

I tried to fasten the seatbelt around her waist. An angry, gutteral sound came from her lungs in protest. I backed away, startled by the noise, which sounded more like an animal in distress than a human being.

“Where do you live?” I asked as I signaled my way back into the traffic. She said nothing. The woman’s suspicious, darting glances alarmed my children in the rear seat.

“Mom?” my daughter called from the back needing reassurance that she and her brother were safe.

“I’m just going to pick up my other daughter from school.” I tried to sound soothing. “Then we’ll find out where you live. ”

A wild snorting, similar to the noise made over the seatbelt, erupted again. Only now it was more vicious, more desperate. My heart raced. What about my waiting child? What about the two seated in back? What kind of jeopardy might I have put us all in?

Her noises were so frightening I obediently passed the school where my child waited. I drove straight ahead until she signaled me to do otherwise. Frantic rappings on the back window with her fingerless hand told me to turn right. Angry, snorting noises said, "You've done something wrong."

Eight miles from the place I'd first seen her we turned into a frozen, rutted driveway. A badly decaying relic from decades past served as home. A child's rusty tricycle was tipped on its side and held comatose in the compacted snow. The metal storm door banged wildly against its frame. Dozens of black, plastic garbage bags posed like eerie frozen statues in the snow-covered yard.

The woman hunched her angular frame into the wind. She watched with piercing intensity as I carried her groceries to the door. Before I reached my car again, she slammed the metal door shut without a word.

This good deed didn't feel so good. What was I looking for? A thank-you from a woman unable to even tell me where she lived? A pat on the back? An "atta girl"?

Love is often untidy. Real love, not Hollywood fluff stuff. It is firm, unchangeable, and hard. It is often missing that feel-good quality we human beings are perennially on the prowl for. Real love isn't tidy. In fact it's downright messy. Real love doesn't pass by the unlovely in pain. Real love doesn't look for a thank-you. It is its own reward.

Jesus loved a man who would eventually sell him out for a bit of silver. He loved him as much as the other eleven who didn't sell him out. He loved the Pharisees enough to tell them the truth about their spiritual condition. You are like whitewashed tombs, he said, looking good on the outside but filled with a bunch of rattly bones on the inside.

Jesus loved two violent, demon-possessed men who caused others to turn aside in fear and disgust. He loved a lonely, old woman missing some fingers and probably a tongue by sending her help in a blizzard. He loved a common mother of three enough to show her what real love is.

The Health of Christ

LAURA MOMARY

"It's strange being the one everyone is praying for," my sister confided to me one night over the phone. It was true—my sister was usually the praying one, not the one people prayed for. But since she had developed severe muscle pain, swollen lymph nodes, fatigue, and migraines several months before, my mother had emailed, called, and written to everyone she knew, asking them to pray.

The four doctors my sister had visited had been less than encouraging, regretfully telling her that her symptoms were very difficult to diagnose and that she would have to go through several blood tests before they could discover the cause and name of her illness. Several blood tests became months of blood tests, and her condition worsened. New mysterious symptoms, such as rashes and cold sores, would come and go, and although the doctors still could not make a definite diagnosis, lupus and fibromyalgia were the most likely possibilities.

Joanna was not used to illness and tried to continue living as if hers was nonexistent. We all admired her strength; rarely did she complain. But soon she had to quit her job in order to get more rest, and her activities were limited by the soreness of her muscles. The doctors, after five months, still had no diagnosis, and my mother faithfully kept her email and church friends informed and praying.

During one of my sister's visits to me in Chicago, we attended an Episcopal service in a nearby suburb. She sat quietly on the hard wooden pew, occasionally lifting her hand to scratch the rash on her neck. The priest slowly proceeded through the liturgy, and we knelt for the Prayers of the People and lifted the names of those suffering with illness or disease, as he directed. In my mother's faint whispers I heard my sister's name repeatedly, and Joanna's husband took Joanna's hand.

At the administration of Communion, we came before the altar at the front of the church. "This is the body of Christ sacrificed for us," the priest repeated softly as he broke the bread for each of those kneeling for Communion. As he stood before my sister, he placed the bread of Christ in her hands and said to her, "The health of Christ is yours."

We didn't know how the priest knew my sister was ill; I had not been at the church long enough for him to even recognize my name. "But we have to believe that you've been healed, Jo-Jo. It might take your body a while to catch up, but God has healed you!" Mom's faith encouraged all of us, and we left the church believing that the Great Physician had healed my sister.

Two months after the service at St. Mark's, the most recent batch of blood tests came back negative, and Joanna's symptoms have disappeared.

I am continually overwhelmed with the sovereignty God holds over the illnesses of our world as I think about the healing hand he laid on my sister. It is two thousand years after Christ's ministry on earth, and he still heals, he still answers prayer, and he still gives his people glimpses of the grace that is yet to come.

Lonely Garden

CORRIE TEN BOOM

[Here, Corrie ten Boom, imprisoned in a concentration camp for harboring persecuted Jews in World War II, is allowed to walk outside for the first time in weeks.]

The gate was a bolted door and when I had gone through it, I was once *again alone.* After nine weeks, this was my first time outside. Red flowering shrubs, colorful little primroses, grass, yellow dunes, and a wide blue sky. My legs were stinging from their unfamiliar movement, but I walked and walked, and I drank in the colors and the air. Tremendous emotion made my heart beat faster, and then an unspeakable melancholy descended within me. I saw the colors through my tears. In me and around me was more loneliness than in the cell, and all of a sudden I did not see any beauty in the bare yard, but an atmosphere of death and cruelty.

Behind the south wall the rattle of a machine gun broke the silence. Then everything was, again, terrifyingly quiet. It was two o'clock and it was as if everything around me were a ghost city and I the only one alive. I walked on and an uncontrollable homesickness surged up in my heart.

Suddenly I remembered Enoch in the Bible. He was not filled with homesickness when he walked with God and so I was no longer alone either. God was with me. Hand in hand, we walked on and saw the blue sky and the flowers and the flowering shrubs, and I could see the yard as a part of a beautiful free world where I would be allowed to walk once again. In the same way, earth is a lonely garden and heaven is where great joy awaits us children of the Light.

When God Says No

I am full of hope that when God delays

in fulfilling our little thoughts,

it is to have Himself room to work out His great ones.

LILIAS TROTTER, A PASSION FOR THE IMPOSSIBLE

CHAPTER FOUR

The Grace of No

Sometimes, what seem to be God's harsh refusals are really signs of grace.

"Hush, God Is in It"

LAWRENCE CRABB, SR. AND LARRY CRABB, JR.

At a young age, my father was a victim of the deadly flu epidemic of 1917. Years later, my mother described in her own words what happened when he died:

> I was sitting beside the bed. Somehow I knew this was the end, and for the first time I cried in front of you children. God was taking my Charlie after giving us so short a time together. He was leaving me a widow with four children. What was I to do? Then [Charlie] looked at me. He recognized me, and I saw all the tenderness again in his eyes. He sat up and put his arms around me. For a moment I thought he was going to get well. Then he said, "Laura, Laura, don't cry. *Hush, God is in it.*" Then he was gone.

Papa's dying words made no sense to me, his five-year-old son. God's unpredictability was anything but delightful to me. But now, those words bring enormous comfort to that same boy, over seventy-five years later. And they helped sustain my mother during fifty lonely years of widowhood. Just before my mother died, her heart failed and she was unable to speak. Yet somehow, she mustered her last bit of strength and gasped one word: "Hush." Her husband's dying words remained with her through all those years and were on her lips as she went to be with him.

The Bus That Would Not Stop

PATRICIA ST. JOHN

"Wake up, Fatima, we must be starting; the sun is already over the crest of the hill!"

Fatima yawned and sat up. She and Mary had been sleeping in the village where they went every Tuesday evening to give out medicine and to tell the gospel message to any who wanted to hear. Menana, a woman whom Mary had first met in her dispensary, had begged them to come and had gladly welcomed them into her little home. Each Tuesday at sunset the thatched hut filled up with a crowd of dark-eyed villagers on their way home from the fields. Some wanted medicine only, but some would stay on, crouched 'round the charcoal, asking for Bible stories. Sometimes they would discuss a question far into the night, and it was often after midnight when they lay down to sleep on the mattresses lining the walls.

Nevertheless, Fatima and Mary had to be up early and get back home as fast as they could, for children arrived at about nine o'clock for school. Sometimes the two walked the eight-mile distance, but occasionally they caught a rather irregular market bus that would take them about three miles on their way, to a certain fork in the road.

That early summer morning they started off as usual. The harvest had been reaped, and the fields were pale gold stubble. The dawn wind stirred the threshing floors. Down by the river the Indian corn grew in emerald patches, and the figs were ripe for picking. The sky was already bright through the early mists, and they could tell it was going to be very hot. The sooner they got home the better. To their great relief, the bus, laden with villagers, was in sight as they reached the main road. They managed to squeeze in.

Soon Fatima nudged Mary, for they were getting near the fork in the road. They rose and battled their way to the front.

"Stop, please," called out Fatima. "We want to get off here."

But the driver turned out to be a very surly, unpleasant man. He replied, "I am not going to stop here. This is no proper stopping place. I'm going on to the next bridge. There is another fork there, and you can walk back to your village."

"But that will take us miles out of our way down the valley!" cried Mary. "It will take us hours to walk back up that steep mountainside. Oh, please stop!" And in her heart she cried to God, *Oh Lord, we need to get home, and it is getting so hot. Please make him stop.*

But the driver would not be persuaded, and there was nothing to do but to go and sit down again. Mary felt very cross indeed, but Fatima was surprisingly calm. "We prayed this morning that all would be well," she said. "We shall get back some time. Let us be patient."

When at last the bus stopped and put them down at the foot of a steep hill seven miles from home, Mary did not feel at all patient. They stood gazing down the valley hoping another vehicle would appear, but there was nothing in sight. Already the heat was shimmering on the hills, and the river, almost dried up now, trickled between the oleander bushes.

Fatima and Mary never heard the woman approaching. She had walked down the hill behind where they stood, and in her arms was a bundle covered with a cloth. She glanced at Mary, but went straight to Fatima. "Is that the English nurse?" she demanded.

"Yes, my sister," replied Fatima.

"Then present me to her," said the woman.

She was a strong country woman in a shady straw hat, with a striped cloth round her waist. On her legs she wore leather gaiters to protect her from thorns and snake bites, and round her neck she wore charms to protect her from evil spirits. She came straight over to where Mary stood and drew the cloth away from the bundle in her arms. It was a baby whose face she had covered to keep the flies away from its infected eyes. The lids were swollen as large as purple grapes, and they were stuck shut. What the eyes were like underneath had yet to be discovered.

"I have brought her to you," said the woman simply.

"How long has she been like that?" asked Mary.

"Four days. She lies crying with her face to the wall and will not suck."

"But how did you know to come here? It is not market day. There are no others from your village on the road."

"Last night I knew my child was getting worse. She was burning with fever. I slept with a heavy heart, and as I slept, I dreamed. A man came to me dressed all in white and he said to me, 'Take that child to the English nurse.'

"I said in my dream, 'I do not know where she lives, nor do I know her.'

"And the man in white answered, 'Rise at dawn and go down to the main road by the bridge, and there you will find her waiting for you. She will tell you what to do.'

"So I came and you are here."

The three women set off up the long hill, and soon another bus came and picked them up, making their journey much shorter. The mother stayed with Fatima and Mary all day, and by evening, after penicillin injections and frequent irrigations, her baby looked much better. Then Mary sent medicine home with her and promised to visit on the next Saturday.

The child recovered completely, and the Saturday visit was only the first of many opportunities to speak to that family and village about the love of Jesus. And sitting on the floor that day talking with the mother and her neighbor about the Savior's love, Mary and Fatima thanked God many, many times that he had answered *wait* when Mary had prayed that the bus would stop.

The Same Brown Eyes

EDITH SCHAEFFER

Amy Carmichael always counted her earliest memory of prayer as the time when at the age of three she prayed most earnestly that her brown eyes would be changed by God to blue and then climbed up on a chair in the early morning to look disappointingly into the mirror and find the same brown eyes. At that early time she was taught and kept it as a part of her prayer life's warp and woof that answers to prayer are "no" and "wait," as well as "yes."

Circuitously, she ended up a missionary in India, affecting the lives of thousands of children. Her brown eyes and dark hair, which helped her to move among the market places in her Indian sari and sandaled feet (having stained her skin brown to be less noticed), were God's provision. The Lord's answer was in the "no" to her request for "blue eyes like the skies." She was needed in India and her brown eyes were the best equipment. This story she repeated to her beloved Indian children many years later.

The Naked Man

KIM BOLTON WITH CHRIS WAVE

Tony (my husband) and I worked out a nocturnal tag-team operation with all four of our children. I took the first shift (10:00 P.M. to 3:00 A.M.). He took the second shift (3:00 A.M. to 7:00 A.M.). This arrangement gave me hope. Thinking I might sleep four hours straight saved me from despair.

On this particular night, I was snuggled in between my sheets. It was ten minutes before ten o'clock. I was praying and praying because I remembered what my mother always taught me: "If you can't fall asleep, you need to pray. The devil doesn't want you to pray so he'll leave you alone and let you go to sleep." I know this isn't Scripture, but it works for me.

"Lord, please let me sleep. Let all of these children sleep on my shift. If they have to wake up, let it be on Tony's shift."

The baby woke on my shift. I staggered off in the direction of the wailing baby. I rocked and swayed with the baby. I sang, patted, and prayed for ninety minutes. Ninety long minutes.

I sang:

Jesus loves me this I know.
You should be asleep, you know. . . .
Go to sleep, Baby.

Ninety minutes. I was thinking about an injection, a pill, anything I could get my hands on to make this child go to sleep. At three o'clock in the morning mothers are not praying anointed prayers.

Jesus loves me this I know.
Go to sleep, Baby, and we'll all know . . .

I wanted my bed and nothing more. I would not be able to handle tomorrow if I did not get into bed soon.

Three-thirty A.M. I crawled back to bed, wasted.

Please, no, it can't be. I heard the other one coming down the hall. I threw back the covers and patted the bed. "Come on, just get in bed with me," I said without turning to look at her.

She wouldn't budge. I could hear her breathing, but she wouldn't move. I thought, *Okay kid, go ahead and sleep on the floor, but you're gonna freeze.*

A few minutes later, I said it again, "Come on, get in bed with me. It's cold."

No movement. Only breathing.

Finally, that mother gene kicked in, and I thought she needed to be off the cold floor. I said, "Please get in bed with me, now." I turned over to look at her only to discover that this was not my child. It was a man. It was a naked man.

He was down on all fours, naked, and covered with whipped cream. He was so close, I could almost touch him.

I pinched my own left hand with my right to make sure I was really awake and not dreaming. I was awake.

"What in the world are you doing here?" I asked out loud.

I reached behind me to shake Tony into consciousness, calling him in a screaming whisper as I kept my eyes on the naked man, "Tony . . . Tony . . . Tony!" I shook him hard. He turned a sleepy eye in my direction and said, "What's your sister doing here?" (The only thing my sister has in common with this man is that they are both blond.)

"That's not my sister," I whispered.

"Who is it?"

"I don't know."

"What is it?"

"It's a naked man in our room!" We were chit-chatting about this froth-covered man who was listening to every word we said, still down on all fours. His behind was in the air and his head was on the floor. Tony and I were discussing his presence after I'd asked him to get in bed with me—three times!

Suddenly, the naked man freaked. He grabbed the phone and zinged it at Tony's head. Blood started gushing in every direction. And the man ran off.

We checked under beds and in closets to see if he was working in tandem. Was there another whipped cream–covered man somewhere in my house? Satisfied he came alone, we called the police. The naked man was long gone.

The police finished their report and I was left with a different house. This was now a house someone evil had entered uninvited, leaving fear in his wake. This somebody knew how I slept. He knew where my children slept. He knew what I wore to bed and what I kept in my refrigerator. I couldn't get beyond the violation left by his intrusion. While I had rocked my sleepless baby, he had plundered my things. He ransacked my house. He tore up my kitchen. He pulled out all the phone lines (preparing for what?).

I was unable to sleep through the night anymore. I started doing laundry at all kinds of crazy hours.

Two weeks later, I was shaking out a sheet from the dryer at two o'clock in the morning. I looked up and saw the front door handle turn. This time I yelled. Tony came running. The guy ran off, but the locks had been chiseled off the front door.

Somebody's after me. Somebody's after my kids. What's he going to do to us when he gets us? Why does he want me? All the locks in the world won't keep him out. What am I going to do? I can't get away. These thoughts continually ran through my head.

Drowning in fear, I stopped sleeping altogether. I became bitter and judgmental. I blamed Tony for not protecting me. I said to him in anger, "If you're such a great husband, why didn't you get that guy and kill him? Why didn't you run after him?"

No one hurt as I did. No one knew how I was feeling. Fear strangled all my reason and perspective. I was caught in its jaws and couldn't get loose. It was ransacking my life.

Six weeks into this nightmare, Tony came to me, put his hands on my shoulders and said, "You'd better get 'hold of God. You're going crazy, and you're driving the rest of us crazy too."

I turned away from him; I was in pain. But later, alone in my room, I realized he was right. I cried out to God. I turned to the back of The Book. I looked under the index listings for *fear, peace,* and *sleep,* because those words were huge in my mind. I didn't have an ounce of peace and I hadn't slept in six weeks. I wrote down on a 5 x 7 sheet of paper every verse listed in the back of The Book.

"What time I am afraid, I will trust in Thee." "Fear not, for I am with thee." "I will keep in perfect peace those whose minds are stayed on Me." "When you go through the fire, you will not be burned and when you go through the waters you will not drown." "I will lie down and sleep in peace." "Your sleep will be sweet and you will dwell in safety." "He will give his angels charge over you." "I will never leave you or forsake you." "I will not relax my hold on you." "I will not fail you." "You can boldly and with confidence say, 'the Lord is my helper.'"

I didn't believe a word of it. But I wrote all those verses down. I kept that slip of paper in my pocket by day. I lay down every night with those verses on my chest. I asked God to permeate my being with those verses. I said those verses out loud, believing that faith would come by hearing and hearing by the Word of God. My mouth said them and my spirit heard them.

Slowly, over a stretch of time, my faith increased. God was healing me. Three months after those incidents, I woke up with a new interpretation of the event. The facts remained the same. What had changed was how I saw those facts.

A naked man broke into my house, I thought. *He was so close I could have touched him. He walked by my girls' rooms. He could have taken them, molested them, or killed them. He came into my room, kneeled right by my bed. The miracle is, he could not touch me. He could not touch my children. The second time he came, he couldn't even get in the door. He was powerless.*

Psalm 91:11-12 says God will give his angels charge over you. They will lift you over the rock so you don't dash your foot against it. I had a boulder in my life. A boulder of fear and doubt. The angels of God lifted me over it.

Clinging

KATE KRUSE

My husband and I weren't sure we wanted to have kids, but when we were in our mid-thirties we started rethinking it. After considering it a couple of months, we decided yes. I got pregnant the next month. There are lots of people who have a hard time getting pregnant, so we were shocked that I got pregnant so quickly.

We were happy about the good news of the pregnancy. I started to write out my thoughts to the baby and to myself to explain what I was experiencing. The first two months I wrote in that journal about my joy, how excited I was that I was pregnant. I thanked God for his generosity and timing. I wrote too, about my fears of miscarriage. I felt weak about that, but believed God's strength could keep me strong.

In August I wrote down in my journal how excited I was that the baby would be the size of a pea by now. That was the last entry for months.

Out of the blue, I dove into a depression. I knew that I was going through hormonal changes. I had struggled with depression in the past. But now this inescapable dark feeling hovered over me—surprising and upsetting me because I had been so excited about the baby.

It was then that I experienced the hardest four months of my life. Those were the lost months. I was so depressed that I didn't want to live—and I felt depressed about those feelings, guilty about those feelings, because I had a little life inside me. There were months of silence in my journal.

I couldn't see any hope. I couldn't visualize a joyful life with my baby in the future. I just cried a lot and wanted to stop feeling the pain I was feeling. Then, after a few months I sought professional help for the depression.

In the middle of this time I had a feeling of bleak darkness, and I asked God to replace it with his light and hope. I asked God to forgive me and to help me move forward. God seemed distant and quiet. I asked him why I didn't feel better, why he wouldn't take away the pain.

Cling to God became my daily phrase. I knew that God was good, and I had to choose to believe that and keep coming to him.

Slowly a change came. In January I wrote in my journal that I felt encouraged about God's faithfulness. I found how life-changing *clinging to him* was. I couldn't see the future and be encouraged. But just trying little by little, every day, I told God, "I will believe this about you, I will believe that you are faithful."

I clung to the verses in Psalm 34: "I prayed to the Lord, and he answered me, freeing me from all my fears. Those who look to him for help will be radiant with joy; no shadow of shame will darken their faces" (vv. 4-5, NLT).

I memorized that. I wrote it on a card and carried it with me everywhere I went. For months I read and prayed that same psalm.

Now my baby girl is ten months old and my life is fuller than it ever has been. I am able to testify about God's faithfulness. During my months of depression, God made it very obvious to me that quietly throughout the day, stopping in the middle of whatever I was doing, I could cling to him and he would be faithful. He tangibly continued to care for me through the love and prayers of family and friends.

There's a psalm now that I turn to, Psalm 103: "Praise the Lord, I tell myself, and never forget the good things he does for me" (v. 2, NLT). Someone once told me a paradox: There's a time when God doesn't seem to be around, but when you come through that hard and lonely time, you know there's no one else who brought you through it.

That's how it was for me.

Many Mansions

DORIE FINK

I was teaching fourth grade at a religious elementary school. The third week of class, one of the pupils told us, "Last night at dinner, my mom told us that she can stop taking one of her medications. Please pray that she will soon be able to stop taking all of her medicine." Zach's mom, Mary, had been battling cancer for some time. Most recently she had been struggling with stress to her heart due to complications from her chemotherapy treatment. Zach had watched his mother go in and out of the hospital several times and knew the seriousness of her situation. With great courage he had shared much about his mother's illness with his classmates, and they often anticipated his requests for prayer.

The following morning, Zach's mom died. She had had a good morning, even making the children's lunches and signing their assignment notebooks, something she had done only once before that school year. She died a peaceful death, in her sleep, while Zach sat in my classroom. The impact of her death hit me hard. How could I care for her little boy? What words could I possibly speak to his classmates? And what about Zach's father and two younger brothers?

During the weeks leading up to Mary's death, we had spent a lot of time in class talking about heaven. What will heaven be like? How can we get there? What will we be able to do in heaven? During all of our discussions, I kept a special eye on Zach. Though he never voiced any concern, I knew he must be wondering if his mom would experience the realities of heaven any time soon. I don't think any of us had expected it to be so soon.

As we had talked about heaven, we had memorized John 14:2: "In my Father's house are many mansions. . . . I go to prepare a place for you" (NKJV). We had even learned a song for that verse and had spent two weeks preparing to sing it in chapel. During each rehearsal, I reminded the kids that we were going to be singing this for all of the other students at our school because we needed to remind each other of this wonderful promise from God. Little did I know how much we would need to claim that promise ourselves. But God knew. It was the day before we were to sing it publicly that Mary died.

The night of Mary's death, Zach and his father and brothers grieved together. The following morning, Zach was in school. He had decided that was what he wanted, and his father wisely went along.

The plan was that Zach would meet us in chapel so that I would have a few minutes alone with his classmates to tell them of Mary's death.

I will never forget taking the final step into the classroom that day. I told the children that I had something very important to tell them. A hush fell over the room as they settled into their seats and turned to look toward me. As my eyes filled with tears, twenty fourth graders waited to hear what I had to say. Swallowing hard, I reminded them of the reasons for our singing in chapel and why John 14:2 was such good news.

I then told them that Zach's mom had died and that she now had one of those mansions. As I looked across the classroom, I saw strained faces that before this had hardly been touched by death. It didn't take long for someone to note that Mary no longer had to take her medicine, and that is what we had prayed for.

Minutes later, as I stood and watched those fourth graders sing, I realized that God had done more than answer our prayers that Mary could stop taking her medicine. God had answered prayers that we hadn't even known to pray—prayers that each one of us, in different ways, would be equipped to deal with this loss.

Mary's death was not easy. Her family continues to work through their grief. But God had prepared us to claim his promises. To my ears, the voices of the children sounded like angels that morning. And I'm sure that the heavenly choirs surrounding Mary's new mansion joined in.

Miracle on 10th Street

MADELEINE L'ENGLE

A snapshot of a little girl, a piano, a Christmas tree. What could be more ordinary, more normal, more safe? But it wasn't safe that Christmas. It might have been ordinary and normal, because what happened to us happens to many people, but it wasn't safe!

This little girl, our first child, is looking wistfully at the tree, and her usual expression was vital, mischievous, full of life. But that Christmas she was wilted, like a flower left too long without water. She sat with her toy telephone and had long, quiet conversations with her lion ("You can never talk while the lion is busy," she would explain). She didn't run when we took her to the park. She was not hungry. I bathed her and felt her body, and there were swollen glands in her groin, her armpits.

We took her to the doctor. He looked over our heads and used big medical words. I stopped him.

"What you are saying is that you think she has leukemia, isn't it?" Suddenly he looked us in the eyes. When he knew that we knew what he feared, he treated us with compassion and concern. We knew the symptoms because the child of a friend of ours had died of leukemia. We knew.

We took our little girl to the hospital for tests, and she was so brave that her very gallantry brought tears to my eyes. We went home to our small apartment and sat in the big chair and told stories and knew that we would have several days' wait for the test results because of the holidays.

My husband was an actor. I am a writer. Like most artists, we had vivid imaginations. We tried hard not to project into the unknown future, to live right where we were, in a small apartment on 10th Street in New York City. We loved our apartment, where we slept on a couch in the living room. To get to the bedroom we had to walk through the kitchen and then the bathroom. At that time Leonard Bernstein lived on the top floor and would occasionally knock on our door to leave his suitcases when he did not want to make the long climb up the stairs. We were happy. My husband was playing on Broadway. I had had two books published and was working on a third. We had a beautiful child.

And suddenly the foundations rocked beneath us. We understood tragedy and that no one is immune. We remembered a church in New England where, carved in the wood of the lintel, are the words: REMEMBER, NO IS AN ANSWER.

My mother grew up in a world of Bible stories, and I thought of the marvelous story of Shadrach,

Meshach, and Abednego. These three young men refused to bow down to an idol, a golden image, and King Nebuchadnezzar was so furious that he ordered them to be thrown into a furnace so hot that the soldiers who threw them into the fire were killed by the heat.

But Shadrach, Meshach, and Abednego stood there in the flames, unhurt, and sang a song of praise of all creation.

King Nebuchadnezzar was astonished and asked, "Did we not cast three men bound into the fire?" They answered, "True, O King." He replied, "But I see four men loose, walking in the midst of the fire, and they are not hurt, and the appearance of the fourth is like the Son of God."

And that, perhaps, is the most astounding part of the whole story. God did not take Shadrach, Meshach, and Abednego out of the fiery furnace. God was in the flames with them.

Yes, it is a marvelous story, but I thought, *I am not Shadrach, Meshach, or Abednego, and the flames burn.*

I rocked my child and told her stories and prayed incoherent prayers. We turned on the lights of the Christmas tree, lit a fire in our fireplace, turned out all the other lights, and I managed to sing lullabies without letting my voice break or tears flow. When my husband got home from the theater we put her to bed, and we held each other. We knew that the promise had never been safety or that bad things would not happen if we were good and virtuous. The promise was only that God would be in it with us, no matter what it is.

Even before the test results came from the hospital our little girl began to revive, to laugh, to wriggle as we sat together on the piano bench to sing carols. Our hearts began to lift as we saw life returning to her, and the tests when they were returned indicated that she had had an infection. It was not leukemia. She was going to be all right. She is now a beautiful young woman with children of her own, and she has gone through her own moments of terror when her eldest child was almost killed by a car. I suspect that most parents know these times. I know that the outcome is not always the one we pray for. In my own life there have been times when the answer has indeed been no. My husband died, and I will miss him forever. This past July the car I was in was hit by a truck and I was almost killed. I am still recuperating and wondering by what miracle my life was saved, and for what purpose. Certainly everything is more poignant. Were the autumn leaves this year more radiant than usual? What about the tiny new moon I saw last night? And my family and my friends: Have I ever loved them as much as I love them now?

I think back to that Christmas when my husband and I did not know whether our little girl would live to grow up.

Between that Christmas and this there have been many times when I have been in the fiery furnace, but I am beginning to understand who is in there with me and that when I need it, I am given courage I never knew I had. Every day is a miracle, and I hope that is something I will never forget.

Wren Song

The song came, it seemed,
To split my heart open
Like the ice,
Cracking off trees,
Like branches breaking
In all this cold
And darkness.
How can there be such a song
Without pain?
Why did the wren sing
In the sleet
Before the light came?

ANNE KEITH

CHAPTER FIVE

The Grace of Letting Go

Sometimes holding too tightly to our own ideas
leaves no room for God's grace.

Da Big Chair

KIM BOLTON WITH CHRIS WAVE

God will speak to this people, to whom he said, "This is the resting place, let the weary rest"; and, "This is the place of repose"—but they would not listen. So then, the word of the Lord to them will become: Do and do, do and do.—Isaiah 28:11–13, NIV

Jelly globs beckoned me to release them from their incarceration to my table. I picked the path of least resistance across my kitchen floor, hoping to avoid the toddler cookie-drool that threatened to glue me in place. Unmade beds, dirty dishes, unopened bills, carpool responsibilities, the needs of my family—what about my needs?

From the middle of the screaming piles, a small, sweet voice beckoned. I peered over the edge of the basket I was carrying—laundry mounded past my eyebrows.

"Hey, Mom," he said. "Why dontcha come and sit wif me in da big chair?"

Balancing my precarious load, I explained to my toddler, "I have too much to do; I can't sit in the big chair or anywhere else, Honey."

"Come on, come and sit wight here by me." He patted the space between him and the arm rest.

"I can't, Baby," I moaned, thinking of the chores that numbered in the legion.

"Come on now; it'll just take a minute, just a wittle minute." He smiled the irresistible smile of a two-year-old boy. He continued to pat the waiting space next to him.

I dropped my load of laundry. I melted into the seat next to him. And he placed his tiny hand on my face and said, "Now, isn't dis nice, Mom?"

"Yes," I said, "it's wonderful." We sat together for ninety seconds.

Then as if he understood the demands waiting for me, he tenderly patted my leg and said, "You can go now."

Just like Jesus. He waits, patting the space next to him and says, "This is the resting place—next to me."

“Maybe tonight,” we say,"maybeafterlunchmaybewhenItakeoutthetrashmaybetonightbeforebed maybetomorrowafterschoolbeforebed." And it doesn’t happen.

He keeps patting.

Jesus keeps patting the space between him and the “next thing,” saying, “Just a little minute. A little minute in My Big Chair. It will change your day, probably your life.”

“Maybebeforebathtime,bedtime,suppertimemaybemaybe,” we drone.

Sit yourself in da big chair. Find your spot in the quiet place. Sit there, so that the Lord doesn’t have to say to you, “O.K. then, ‘do and do, do and do.’”

Arguing with God

DEB CLARKIN

After I graduated from college, I wasn't sure what I wanted to do or where I should live. I needed money and a sense of security, so I got an apartment in the town where I went to college and took a job as an elementary school music teacher. I liked the kids I taught and I had a place to stay, but I was restless and discouraged. My family lived in Minnesota—too far away to visit easily. I often felt lonely.

The hardest thing for me was the nagging feeling that I should move to Minnesota even though I saw no possible way to move. I had no job in Minnesota, no place to stay on my own, and I didn't know a lot of people there. I didn't even know what I would want to do if I moved. Yet as I prayed about the situation, I continually sensed God telling me, "Move."

I argued with God, saying just what my friends and family were telling me—"It's not right to move before you have a job and a place to stay."

Finally, after months of trying to be peaceful when I was actually discouraged, I made plans to move to Minnesota.

Once I made the decision to move, I think I expected everything to fall into place, but it didn't. I interviewed with several organizations but wasn't drawn to any job. I found it harder than I expected to leave where I was, and I wondered if I would be more lonely miles away from my friends. God still said, "Move."

I tried to trust God but was afraid of the future. Nevertheless, I packed my apartment into boxes and left. Then God's answers to my prayers began to come. A close friend from college opened her home to me for as long as I wanted to stay. I accepted a job working with youth in an after-school program. I even found a church I liked.

What was especially good about moving was that I was able to be with my younger sister, who started going through a very difficult time that year. Our mom had died several years before, so my sister especially needed me close. I now saw why God had been urging me to move. I needed to be near my family during that time. I don't think the year I spent waiting to move was wasted, because God gives grace in every circumstance. I did learn, though, that when we are where God wants us to be, his peace is overwhelming.

A Country Hair Washing*

JODI SCHROEDER

I was staying with a pastor's family in the Czech Republic. I was very thankful to be staying there, but often felt tension between the wife, Klara, and me. I liked her, but cultural and personality differences often made both of us feel misunderstood and hurt.

One February, I went with Klara and her children to a cottage in the country. I was looking forward to the fresh air. An added surprise was that Babi, the childrens' grandmother whom I liked very much, arrived after a few days.

The cottage and the village were beautiful. We had only a coal stove for heat, however, and after four days of living, breathing, and sweating coal, I felt grimy. I asked Klara if I might wash my hair.

She quickly remarked that she had too much work to do and had no time to fetch and boil water for that. I quickly said that I would do all of that and bring extra for her also if she would like. Again, the quick retort, "I'm too busy doing everything for all of us, I don't have time to spend on myself."

I could not handle that and ran out the door and up the lane. Was I asking too much? Why did she always turn everything around to make me look bad? The anger throbbed in my head and my pride forced me farther away. I stayed out for over an hour feeling sorry for myself. Everything in me said that I was right and that I had been treated wrongly, but something else in me clung to the fact that God was in control even then. I knew that I had to go back, and decided that I would be humble no matter what else would happen. As I neared the house, the anger came back but I kept walking and prayed that God would guard my mouth. I tried to enter quietly and go back to my bed, but Klara jumped out of the kitchen to intercept me.

"You know I was only joking," she said. I mumbled quietly that I had not understood her. It was awkward, but Babi, the grandmother, was my angel. She slowly got her large frame out of the rocking chair and prepared a basin as she announced that she was going to wash both Klara's and my hair. I was overwhelmed as she poured the warm water over my head and washed my hair for me. Afterwards, I sat close to the warmth of the stove and watched as she did the same for Klara.

For the rest of the afternoon the three of us drank coffee and talked while we waited for our hair to dry. The washing had brought down barriers between Klara and me. But it was also important to me because God did something in me that day. I felt as though the water went right down to warm and cleanse my soul also. Klara and I continued to have some differences for the remainder of my time overseas, but the country hair washing always reminded me of God's power to cleanse and reconcile in spite of our dirt and sin.

A Great Lesson Learned

ANDRIEN FARQUHARSON

It was a hard time for me. Two of our five children had developed pneumonia. The doctor allowed them to stay at home because he knew we had three other children to care for. I was pregnant with our sixth. It was three days before Christmas. My parents were coming to spend the holiday with us, and we received the news that a family from Mexico City would soon arrive to share Christmas with our family. This would be interesting to work out because my husband and I had a three bedroom house—five children, my parents, Jose and Maria and their two girls, and my husband and I. Because I had bought Christmas presents for all, money was in short supply. How was I going to feed everyone? I was really concerned and did a lot of pacing back and forth.

Then the saddest thing of all happened. I had a miscarriage. After a call to the doctor, I had to drive myself to the hospital, for we couldn't leave the children alone. Someone had to give the two with pneumonia special attention.

As I headed out the door, the phone rang. It was our friends from Mexico wanting directions to our house. My husband gave me a kiss goodbye and began giving directions. I cried all the way to the hospital and felt really sorry for myself.

In the hospital they couldn't seem to decide where I should be. They sent me to three different places. After being told at the third place that I should go back to the first place, I sat down on a bench in the hall and began to sob. *God, I can't do this anymore. Do whatever you want with me. I'm so tired I can't do this anymore.*

Only a few minutes passed and I looked up and saw my doctor coming down the hall with a wheelchair. Nurses and aides were following him, offering to push the chair for him. "No!" he answered. "I will get my patient to the right place myself." That doctor will always be special to me because he cried with me as we talked about my miscarriage.

God was so gentle and tender with me. The greatest sense of peace I have ever known filled me. Neighbors heard about my miscarriage and began to bring food—lots of food. Maria and her family arrived at our house and began to care for our children. My husband was able to come to the hospital to be with me. When my parents arrived the next day, all was peaceful and every need was met. Praise God. I learned a great lesson. When I let go—really let go, take my hands off—then God answers my needs in ways more gentle, more loving, and more powerful then I can even imagine. Thank you, Father.

I'm Not in Charge

JUDY JOHNSON

One day when I was tired of "life in the fast lane," I went to a park and sat in the silence and asked God to speak to me. I thought about how beautiful the day was—the sun, the trees, the lake, the birds—and then God spoke to me through those things, telling me that I was part of his creation with the same beauty. I hadn't thought about being beautiful like the rest of God's creation. For the first time I saw my identity as part of creation in a new way. I now began to understand why it was so important for me to spend time outside. I was part of God's good creation: beautiful, strong, and ever-changing.

I've never been one to want to spend much time in the back woods, so I never thought of myself as "outdoorsy." But I came to see how important being near nature was to me. Everything in me wanted to be near that of which God made me a part.

Usually when I am silent, I wander off into planning, thinking of ways to respond to events happening around me, deciding who I need to talk with that week. Even when I stay focused on listening to God, I usually analyze what I see and hear. I respond right away in some form—or start planning to tell someone what I'm learning. (Some would say I have very few thoughts that don't cross my lips first!) It's hard to let go and not fly into mental action.

The challenge for me is to find ways to continue meeting God so that I can hear his voice anew even when I'm back to my daily routine of work and other responsibilities. God is always ready, but I need to listen. In silence that day in the park, I learned that something is happening, a good thing that God's given me a part in, and I don't *need* to be in charge.

Epiphany

LUCI SHAW

All my life I'd been urged by spiritual leaders to "yield," to "surrender" to God, to "relinquish" my idols. Through overuse those words had lost their impact and freshness for me, but the wildness, the impulsiveness of the word *abandon* challenged me.

One Tuesday morning, a friend encouraged me to rethink my idea of abandonment. He came into my office, sat down, and said, almost without preamble, "I know that often in your life you have felt abandoned—by a father who was away preaching most of the time, by uncaring friends, now by Harold, whose death has left you alone, and by God. I believe that you will only find an answer to your sense of abandonment in *self-abandonment,* in willingness to give away to God your self, your identity. You've been walking through a long, black tunnel. Soon you will see light ahead of you, and when you come out of the tunnel you'll find yourself on the edge of a cliff. *You must throw yourself off the cliff edge and trust that God will catch you in his arms."* Startling words. They made me shiver because I had indeed felt the chill of that abandonment. But they also brought me the tingle of anticipation. I knew I needed to take this wise friend's words seriously. I needed to think through all the implications of his message from God to me, with its prophetic ring, so that I would know *how* to throw myself off the cliff.

On Tuesdays, people at Regent, the college where I teach, meet in small groups to pray and grow together in friendship. Journal in hand, I went to my car with Laurie, a young mother, her baby, and the baby's stroller, which I had to load into the trunk. We drove to the home where our group met, and when I got there I realized with a sick jolt of panic that the journal was gone.

Frantic, I rushed back to the campus in the car and checked in my office, then followed my trail through the building and out again to the parking lot. No journal. As I walked back to my car in the rain, I felt the interior tremor, the recognition of what this event really meant. My journal is an extension of me, as important as arm or leg. In it I feel my life condensed, myself embodied: my most personal observations and ideas and reflections are expressed and recorded in it in a way intensely valuable to me as a tracking of my life. I could buy another new, blank journal and start in again to reflect on its pages, but to lose this one, three-quarters full, was like losing myself. *Losing my self* . . . Suddenly I knew what was happening—God was pressing in for my gift. He was telling me the *how* of abandonment.

I gulped, then found myself saying, inwardly, *This is almost too painful to contemplate, but yes, if my journal stands for what you want from me, I'll give it up to you. I'll abandon it, and throw myself off the cliff edge. But oh, please be there to catch me!*

Still shaking, I drove back to the prayer group. As I pushed open the front door, Laurie met me and said, beaming, "Karen Cooper just phoned to say she'd found your journal in a puddle in the middle of University Avenue. You can pick it up at her house this afternoon." I realized that as I drove away from Regent it must have fallen off the top of the car, where I'd put it while stowing the stroller in the trunk.

Later, when Karen, my student and friend, handed the soggy journal back to me, there was a tire print stippled across its familiar, ugly, orange front cover; its back cover was half ripped off; and the coiled binding of its spine was bent and flattened. But it had been given back to me. I had made the jump. God had made the catch.

Karen and I prayed our exhilaration and thanks. She wondered aloud to me: "And some people doubt the personal involvement of God in their lives? Why should I, who knew you so well, and knew where to call you, be the one to stop my car in the rain, to find out what it was that had caught my eye, lying in that puddle? Why did I stop at all? Traffic was heavy. There were scores of cars and bicycles and pedestrians traveling on that busy street. But I found the journal and saw your name was written on the front."

In the same journal that night I wrote the story, and its conclusion:

If I am willing to abandon my will to God, broken like the spine of this journal, imprinted with God's own tire-track signature, he will give it back, and my identity with it. Oh, I feel it so profoundly, pierced to the core with its reality. God does care for me. He has not abandoned me. I have been "knocked breathless by his powerful glance." He showed himself, beaming his light to my heart in a true epiphany.

On Eagles' Wings

ALICE FRYLING

Becoming a mother surprised me. I was not surprised by the endless diapers, the sleepless nights, or the tiring days. I had anticipated those. But I was surprised by how deeply our daughters invaded my heart. I found myself bound to them in emotional and spiritual ways that I had never experienced before.

One morning when our older daughter was in eighth grade, I knew it was time to loosen the deep bonds I had with her as she faced adolescence and adulthood. I came across a passage in Deuteronomy that showed me God understood my dilemma. The passage described God as a mother eagle who shields and cares for her young, then stirs up her nest and spreads her wings to catch the young and carry them on her pinions.

I thought of the pictures I had seen of huge eagles soaring through the sky. I pictured one of those eagles pushing her young out of the nest and then swooping down under them to catch them if they fell. As my daughter entered high school, I realized that my job was to push her out of the nest, with the promise that I would be there if she needed me.

That image helped both my daughter and me throughout her high school, college, and post-college years. Then, the day she brought home the man she would eventually marry, I sensed that the pushing and swooping were over. I had worn out the eagle image and it was time to move on. Again God gave me a comforting and encouraging passage to think about. I read in Luke how the kingdom of heaven was like a seed planted in the yard which grows into a huge pine tree with thick branches, "and the eagles build nests in it." My heart stood still as I heard his Spirit once again whispering to my spirit. It was time for my daughter to begin building her own nest. Just as God watches over every eagle sweeping the horizon, he would watch over my daughter as a new generation began.

The Christmas Train

CHRIS WAVE WITH KIM BOLTON

It was Christmastime and I felt it rising. The tide of frustration was rising. I wanted to scream something and it was not "HO, HO, HO." I hated everything—this strip mall, the town, my house, the traffic, the weather, my life, my hair.

The stores were predictably crowded, the crowd predictably short-tempered. I forged paths through the clusters of bodies, tugging my two small girls behind me. I tried to avoid the Christmas Train that circled around Santa and his battalion of silly elves. I hoped to avoid the jangly bells because I already had jangly nerves, but the force of the crowd propelled us toward the lacquered train and all its Styrofoam decorations.

"Can we please, Mommy? Please? Please, can we ride?"

"I'm sorry, no." I said flatly. "I don't have any money. "

I did have money, but I was too tired to fish it out of my purse. I didn't want to wait for sixty-five toddlers to ride the train in a dizzying circle before mine got on. I didn't want to stand even one minute squashed between sticky little Benny and his Aunt Emma. I wasn't out of money, I was out of patience and precariously close to being out of my mind.

A young, thirty-ish man stood alone next to us watching the circling train without emotion. I wondered why on earth he was here. He seemed not to be waiting for anyone to get off the Christmas Train. He was unencumbered by packages and apparently not planning to shop as the mall was closing soon. This was the last place I'd be standing if I didn't have to be. I tugged at the hands of my now silent and disappointed little girls and turned to cut a path through the crowd. Just as we were heading away, the young man grabbed my hand and pressed a dollar into it.

Without looking at me or showing any emotion, he said, "Please give them a ride."

"Oh, I couldn't—" I began to protest. "I have money. I just—" I opened my purse and reached in for my wallet. In that second, he vanished. Somehow, he slipped through the thickness of the crowd without a sound. Vanished. The crowd swelled into the spot he once occupied.

My girls rode that Christmas Train, pink-cheeked and screeching with delight. Fifty cents a piece to see those smiles. A little bit of heaven in those smiles.

For the grand sum of one dollar, one regular mom purchased a sliver of God, thanks to a stranger.

What Can God Do?

Some of us believe that God is almighty

and can do everything; and that He is all-wise

and may do everything; but that

He is all-love and will do everything—

there we draw back. As I see it, this ignorance

is the greatest of all hindrances to God's lovers.

JULIAN OF NORWICH, THE REVELATION OF DIVINE LOVE

CHAPTER SIX

God's Extravagant Grace

Sometimes when we expect "just a little grace,"
God overwhelms us with abundant gifts.

You Get Her Anything She Wants

VINITA HAMPTON WRIGHT

My eighty-eight-year-old grandmother, over the past few years, has begun to slow down. Yet she puts in her hour every morning, out in her large yard, caring for various flower beds, trees, and birdbaths. A year or two ago, she was fixing a flowerbed and said to the Lord, "Now, Lord, if I just had a few more bricks . . ."

Not long after, there was a hard rain. When Grandmother looked out her front window the next morning, there was something in the yard near the road. Her curiosity got the best of her, so she checked it out.

Yes, what she saw was a bunch of bricks. Years ago, there was a sidewalk out there, and the rain washed all those bricks out of the ground.

Pretty cool, huh?

I think that maybe grandmothers who are faithful to the Lord for decades just build up prayer credits, to the point that—bricks, a car, whatever they need—God just tells the angels, "You get her anything she wants."

Kids' Club

PAMELA MEADOWS

I'd heard about Kids' Clubs in Cambodia, clubs that teach children Bible stories. Living in the Chicago area suburbs, I saw a need for such a club there. In the World Relief office where I work, we serve refugee children through a preschool program and have tutoring for high school students. But we didn't have anything to offer elementary and junior high school students who were refugees. I started praying for God to meet this need, but we ran on a tight budget. I had no clue how it would be financed. I prayed about it for a while and then forgot about it.

A few months after I'd first prayed about the club, God began providing the answer to my prayers. A woman called my boss to ask if World Relief had a club for elementary age kids. When my boss said we didn't, the woman asked how much it would cost to start one. My boss said she didn't know. The caller asked, "Would $10,000 do it?"

Unaware that I had been praying specifically about this, my boss told me about the call and asked me if I could meet with this person. When this woman came to the office, I started telling her about my idea. I envisioned a program that offered tutoring help, crafts, games, and a Bible story. My ideal place for a Kids' Club, I told her, was the Baptist church right next to apartments where many refugees live. At this point she interrupted me.

"I go to that Baptist church. We've been looking for another way to help the refugee families. Wouldn't it be great if you could use the church for your club?"

When World Relief asked the church about it, they loved the idea and were willing to partner with us in developing and hosting the program. So, with the monetary gift and the church facilities, we began a wonderful Kids' Club. Other people in the church have jumped at the chance to help. With all the help, it is a one-to-one or one-to-two volunteer-child ratio—a rare treat in this kind of program.

It is so encouraging to hear the stories of how children from different countries and different religious backgrounds have become Christians through this club. God has been directing this from day one, and we are amazed at his faithfulness. We will trust him to provide the money to continue the club next year, too.

God's Whispers

MIRIAM BLANK

When my father pulled my brother's drowning body from the lake by our house I was less than three years old. I have heard every version of the story from my siblings who actually were old enough to remember. In my mind I can see my father's heroic rescue: Some days I am convinced that I was old enough to remember the event.

Another incident, however, I *was* old enough by all accounts to remember. I was sitting in the driver's seat of our VW van with my two older brothers. My oldest brother was certainly not of driving age (although that never seemed to stop him from trying to drive). He confidently placed the van in neutral and then left my younger brother and me alone while he went in to find Mom and Dad. The van was on a slight slope and began to move. My other brother, as fearful as I, but quicker than I, jumped out and ran inside for help. I did what a seven-year-old does best—I clung to the steering wheel and waited to see what would happen. As the van began moving down the long driveway my mother was the first of the rescue team. She tried to stop the van. But in those days VW vans had little regard for women less than five feet tall. My mother was knocked over. My father ran to the driver's side and jumped in the moving van and ended the saga.

Now (many many years after my legs could easily reach the brake pedal), I remember even other stories of my parents' gracious care and tender kindness. These stories are subtle—easily forgotten or never recalled. How in the evening they sat by my bed and patted my back until sleep finally took me. (Is changing diapers at three in the morning night after night even a story?) How Dad made our breakfast every day before school (most of them were pretty good, too). How Mom insisted on scrubbing the white back into our socks.

When I find God's hand on my life through the example of my parents, I am moved by both the saving drama and the daily bread. To speak of God's spectacular rescue from deadly waters somehow seems easy for me. And there are those stories. Many. Still, it is God's faithful touches that bring me to an almost shy worship before my Creator. Like my parents' love, the promise of God's daily tender care is a whisper that I cannot forget. To speak of it almost makes it seem insignificant, perhaps because it is very personal. Maybe almost as insignificant and personal as a mother's quiet duty in the night to the sound of her child's cry.

A Time for Pearls

MARGARET JENSEN

The Great Depression was in full swing. The cupboard was bare, and we anxiously awaited Papa's pay. Instead of giving the money to Mama, the treasurer had given the check from the church where Papa worked directly to Papa. Usually it was Mama who got the check and doled out street car tokens and an occasional nickel for a cup of coffee. Papa was noted for "giving freely all things." Walking past a jewelry shop, he saw a lovely string of pearls. At the same time, he felt the money in his pocket. Overjoyed at discovering his wealth, he purchased the pearls.

Bowing low, in great respect, he handed her the gift. "Mama, I suddenly realized I had never bought you a present. You have such a beautiful throat, you should wear pearls."

Mama never flinched. Tenderly she thanked him for the generous gift and promised to wear them always. She did! Later she told me, "There is a time and place for everything. Sometimes we need pearls more than potatoes. That was the time for pearls." Mama somehow saw that we survived until next payday.

This Beautiful Contest

UGOLINO DI MONTE SANTA MARIA

[In Ugolino's book, Little Flowers, *he tells the following story about Saint Francis.]*

Saint Francis was with Brother Leo in an isolated place where they could find no breviary for their morning prayers. Francis instructed Brother Leo to respond to his extemporaneous prayers by repeating and affirming what he heard. Leo agreed to do so and told Francis to begin.

The saint then said to himself, "Brother Francis, you are guilty of much sin and ought to go to hell."

Leo answered, "God will do so many good things through you that you will go to heaven."

"Don't say that, Brother Leo! I told you to repeat what I said."

Leo agreed that he would do so the next time.

Beating his breast and crying and sighing, Saint Francis prayed, "Oh Lord God, I have sinned against you and deserve to be damned!"

Brother Leo answered, "Oh Brother Francis, God will distinguish you among the blessed!"

Francis became impatient with Leo. He commanded him under the rule of holy obedience to respond as directed. "Then you, Brother Leo, Little Lamb, say, 'surely you are not worthy of God's mercy!'"

Assured that Leo would speak as he was instructed, Saint Francis knelt and raised his hands toward heaven. He said, "Francis, you are a wicked sinner. How can God have mercy on anyone as bad as you?"

When Brother Leo responded, he said, "God's mercy is infinitely greater than your sins. He will be merciful to you and bless you."

This created a gentle wonder in Saint Francis. He asked Leo, "Brother, why do you break the rule of obedience?"

With much humility and reverence Leo replied, "God knows I have tried to answer as you want, but God makes me say what he likes and not what I like."

They kept up this beautiful contest all night.

Coffee Shop Miracle

MARILYN P. MASON

When Mary (age 10), David (age 9), and Gerard Mason (age 7) returned to America in June of 1973, following their dad's death in Africa (where the family had been involved in medical missions work), they had a strange request. They wanted to see Johnny Cash, their dad's favorite singer.

Early that fall, I took them to see him appear at a theater in Nanuet, New York, as part of a short family vacation. After the show, instead of grins, I noted tears. Why? They didn't get to shake his hand!

I glibly said something like, "If God had wanted you to meet him, he would have worked it out, . . . and he still could." I guess in my own way I was saying, "Give me a break, kids. I did everything I could to please you." Or, maybe I was trying to let them down gently. Whatever, as kids often do, they took me seriously and literally. They prayed all the way back to the hotel that God would work it out.

The next morning, while Mary, Davy, and Gerry were wading and swimming in the pool, I went to the coffee shop overlooking the pool area to figure out how to handle their disappointment when they would realize that their prayer was not going to be answered.

Had I not spent hours the evening before telephoning New York City hotels trying to locate Johnny Cash—to no avail? As if any hotel would reveal the presence of a celebrity to a complete stranger? What won't a parent do to bring a smile to a child's face—let alone three children in the midst of bereavement?

I soon found out. Only the parent in this case was our heavenly Father. Once I stopped staring into the cup of coffee and looked around my immediate surroundings, I saw Johnny Cash's manager and accompanists right there in the coffee shop, seated at a nearby table. Who couldn't recognize Carl Perkins after watching him perform "Blue Suede Shoes" the night before?

I knew what I had to do. I had to muster up the courage, be willing to appear to be a "groupy," and walk over to their table to explain the situation to them. I did, and the men were touched by the story. Together, we made arrangements for the kids to be introduced to Johnny that night. Of all things, he was planning to come to our hotel to eat supper anyway!

Not only did the kids get to shake his hand, but Johnny talked with them for about fifteen minutes, and we got to eat supper at a small table right next to Johnny's!

To be sure, this was no life-or-death issue, but apparently God delighted in answering the kids' believing prayer—and in demonstrating to me what he says in Psalm 34:10: Those of us who reverence the Lord will never lack any good thing.

God and Bluebonnets

JEANIE MILEY

Romancing fields of bluebonnets in the spring is part of living in Texas. Finding the perfect photo spot of pink, red, yellow, and orange wildflowers, scattered among the blue fields, is part of our family history, and so when it was time to commemorate our thirtieth anniversary, my husband and I decided to find a bluebonnet picture to go over our fireplace.

This anniversary was significant. My husband and I were proud of making it to this milestone and wanted to mark the occasion in a special way. We had worked hard to build our long-term marriage. We had been conscious and intentional in shaping a marriage based on equality, trust, mutuality, and respect, and we were excited about this celebration.

The previous five years had handed us some difficult challenges, and we wanted our bluebonnets to signify a victory over those challenges. Circumstances had led us into a long, dark night of the soul. We needed some way to commemorate the sweet, strong sense of overcoming and prevailing. Our bluebonnets would be our statement of gratitude for the past and hope for the future; they would be a reminder of God's grace after a hard winter season of losses and endings.

When we checked into the motel in San Antonio, the desk clerk asked why we were in the city. When my husband told him the occasion, the desk clerk was stunned. "I don't know anyone who's been married thirty years!" he exclaimed. That night, he had flowers and a card signed by the whole staff sent to our room.

On the day of our anniversary, we left our motel room in San Antonio and took off down the River Walk in the cold December sunshine. I headed for a little souvenir shop I'd browsed before, and quickly found a watercolor print that suited my taste and was well within our limited budget. "This one's pretty," I said.

My husband, known for his non-attachment to things, turned his nose up and said, "That isn't nearly good enough." Shocked, I turned around to investigate this man I must not know as well as I thought I did, even after thirty years.

With my husband in the lead, we left that store and spent the day poking around in various shops until finally he entered an art gallery. My heart sank. We were wasting time! What was he thinking? We couldn't afford a piece of art! We still had one more year of college tuition to pay for before we had our three daughters' education, behind us.

Within minutes, he called to me. "This is what I have in mind," he said. *This* was a bluebonnet painting by the famous Texas artist W. A. Slaughter. It was breathtaking indeed. My heart sank more. There was no way we could have a Slaughter painting. We'd never have our bluebonnets!

When we left San Antonio empty-handed, my nose was out of joint. Over the spring and summer, we half-heartedly pursued our bluebonnets, always with the Slaughter painting as the standard for comparison. Having seen the beauty of Slaughter's work, nothing else would ever measure up to his paintings! My husband's patience persisted, however, while my optimism waned.

In the summer, my mother died, adding to the losses that had piled up for us over the past few years. Other stressors increased, and it seemed that in several areas of our lives God was observing his own great silence with us. We were getting better and better acquainted with grief, learning more about letting go than we had ever wanted to know.

In the fall of that year, we had some extra money, and Martus and I agonized over how to use it. Finally, we began to consider the possibility of buying our bluebonnet painting. The idea was so outrageous for us that we finally agreed that the only way we could justify such an extravagance was to designate the painting for all of our anniversaries until the fortieth.

After long years of struggling to meet the financial demands of raising our family, purchasing art was an outrageous act. However, we wanted a bluebonnet painting, we wanted a Slaughter, and we were, after all, coming up on our thirty-first anniversary. But we almost needed permission to do something so frivolous for ourselves!

Finally, the quest for the bluebonnets moved into high gear. I found an art gallery that had Slaughter paintings in Salado. They sent photographs. We selected our favorite and made our plans for a weekend trip. On a chilly, January weekend, we drove from Houston to Salado and checked into the Stagecoach Inn in Salado, where we had spent one night of our honeymoon. We were as nervous as the day we bought our first house!

That night, as I went to sleep, I said, "Oh, God, please ask my mom and dad if it's O.K. for me to buy that painting!" Martus laughed at me, and I laughed at myself.

The next morning, we crossed the street and went into the Salado Gallery. As soon as we saw the painting, we knew it was the most beautiful bluebonnet painting ever! It was so alive and vibrant, just like our marriage and our faith, both now deeply tested by life.

As we had agreed beforehand, we returned to the coffee shop at the Stagecoach Inn to make our final decision. When we walked into the coffee shop, there sat one of my father's friends whom I had not seen in years, a fellow minister who had been in my home many times during my childhood. We greeted each other warmly. He asked what we were doing in Salado, and we told him about our quest of the bluebonnets.

Martus and I retreated to the far side of the coffee shop. We tried to talk ourselves out of the purchase. We told each other we were crazy. Finally, however, one of us said, "Let's do it," and we stood up to leave before we lost our nerve.

I walked over to my father's friend to tell him good-bye. Before I could say anything, he took me by the hand and looked straight into my eyes. "Honey, go buy those bluebonnets," he said. "That would make your mother and daddy so happy. And you and Martus will enjoy them forever."

Was that coincidence . . . or was it the answer to my childlike prayer? Could it be that the One who cared about the lilies of the fields also cared about bluebonnets and grown-up children who needed some gladness in the midst of the winter? Had the One who had seemingly left us on our own, spoken through my father's good friend in the coffee shop at Salado to give his burdened children a message so clear that we couldn't miss it?

Those bluebonnets hang over our fireplace now, and each time I admire them, I am reminded that the same Messenger who showed up in Salado and nudged us toward hope and delight and spring is surely present in all the seasons of our lives. Even winter.

Acknowledgments

Grateful acknowledgment is made to the following publishers:

"Hush! God Is in It" adapted from *God of My Father,* by Lawrence Crabb, Sr. and Larry Crabb, Jr. Grand Rapids, MI: Zondervan, 1994.

"Rats! God's Answer?" adapted from *When People Pray,* by Barbara Griffiths. Singapore: Overseas Missionary Fellowship, 1987.

"One Explosive Sneeze" and "A Time for Pearls" adapted from *First We Have Coffee,* by Margaret Jensen. Nashville, TN: Thomas Nelson, 1993.

"I Can Pray No More" by Charles Price Jones adapted from *Conversations with God: Two Centuries of Prayers by African Americans,* ed. James Melvin Washington. New York: Harper Perennial, 1994.

"Grace Notes," "Mystery," and "Wren Song" taken from *Homecoming* by Anne Keith, © 1996 by Jim Keith. Fairfax, VA: Self-published. Used by kind permission of the copyright holder.

"Miracle on 10th Street" adapted from *Miracle on 10th Street,* © Madeleine L'Engle, 1991. Used by permission of Harold Shaw Publishers.

"Airport Angel" by Rebecca Puntigam adapted from *Women's Spiritual Passages,* © Lucinda Secrest McDowell, 1996. Used by permission of Harold Shaw Publishers.

"Epiphany" by Luci Shaw adapted from *Stories for the Christian Year,* © Chrysostom Society, 1992. Used by permission of Harold Shaw Publishers.

"Winter Chestnut" by Luci Shaw adapted from *WinterSong,* © Harold Shaw Publishers, 1996.

"The Bus That Would Not Stop" and "The Empty Basket" adapted from *Stories to Share,* © Patricia St. John, 1983. Used by permission of Harold Shaw Publishers.

"Lonely Garden" adapted from *Prison Letters,* by Corrie ten Boom. Old Tappan, NJ: Fleming H. Revell, 1975.

"This Beautiful Contest" by Ugolino di Monte Santa Maria (modernized by Bernard Bangley) adapted from *Near to the Heart of God,* © Bernard Bangley, 1998. Used by permission of Harold Shaw Publishers.